Hampton Wood 1970

Warwickshire
Wildlife Trust

Discover wild Warwickshire

A GUIDE TO LOCAL NATURE RESERVES

Edited by Philippa Vigor
Consultant Editor: John Roberts

First published 2007.

British Library-in-Publication Data
A catalogue record for this book is available from the British Library.

10-digit ISBN
1-874357-34-X

13-digit ISBN
978-1-874357-34-6

Designed and published for Warwickshire Wildlife Trust by
The Naturebureau, 36 Kingfisher Court, Hambridge Road, Newbury, Berkshire RG14 5SJ
www.naturebureau.co.uk

Printed by Portland Print, Kettering, Northamptonshire

Contents

Foreword

Having grown up in the Midlands, I still feel a strong connection to the place which inspired my early love and enthusiasm for nature. I have many fond memories of forays into the undergrowth of my family's garden, and the joy and excitement I experienced finding out first hand about the wildlife there. These early encounters fuelled my fascination with the natural environment and led me into a career that has enabled me to travel the world and study the breath-taking diversity of plants and animals which live on planet earth.

My experiences have also highlighted the need for urgent action to protect our natural heritage, and have stimulated my passion to encourage people everywhere to help conserve nature for future generations. It is easy to look at the rest of the world and focus on what they should do, but we all make up part of the bigger picture – and we can all do our bit. Every journey, however long, starts with a single step. We can all help by taking that step, however small.

I applaud the vital work of Warwickshire Wildlife Trust, an organisation that has recognised the fundamental need to protect and enhance the remaining fragments of nature in Warwickshire, Coventry and Solihull – not only through conservation, but crucially through education too. I welcome this Guide, which helps to make some of the best local wildlife sites available for everyone to experience and enjoy. I hope that it encourages you to discover 'Wild Warwickshire' and that it inspires you to conserve the natural beauty on your doorstep.

David Attenborough

Sir David Attenborough

Acknowledgements

Warwickshire Wildlife Trust would like to thank everyone who helped with the production of this book.

Special thanks are due to John Roberts, Author and Consultant Editor, for his dedication, knowledge and endless enthusiasm, and for the countless hours spent with pen in hand. Also to Philippa Vigor, Staff Editor, who has so successfully coordinated the entire project with efficiency and good humour, and the Trust's Editorial Committee for their contribution in completing the guide: volunteers Roger Cadbury, Kay Reeve, David Morphew, Richard Wright, Graham Harrison, Chris Ivin, Barry Whittington, Val Roberts and Stephan Drew, and staff Andy Tasker, Elaine Skates, Zoe Canham, Beth Gardner, Gina Rowe and Sophie Leszczynska.

Thank you also to all volunteer reserve wardens, reserves staff and placement students, whose combined wildlife expertise, knowledge of the nature reserves and assistance contributed greatly to the accuracy and detail of the guide. Special credit is due to Peter Creed and the team at NatureBureau whose expertise and guidance throughout made the whole process much less daunting.

Sincere thanks to the George Cadbury Fund and Roger and Terry Cadbury for their outstanding generosity in funding the design and production costs of the guide book.

Introduction

Welcome to our new full-colour guide to your local nature reserves, designed to help you get the most out of visiting any of these beautiful places. The guide contains up-to-date wildlife information, along with detailed location and site maps and a rating system to help you decide which reserves to visit first.

If you are looking for a nature reserve on your doorstep, you can refer to the map on the inside front cover. If you know the name of a reserve you want to visit, there is an index at the back of the book. We have grouped our nature reserves together in three bands, depending on their size, accessibility and ecological importance. Using our special 'traffic light' colour code, you will find our larger, more special reserves in the green section, our medium reserves in the amber section and our smaller reserves in the red section. Each nature reserve is listed alphabetically within its colour-coded section.

Whether you follow our rating system or your own preferences, we advise that you check the site description before making your visit. We have tried to ensure that you have enough information to find our reserves, whether by public transport, car, bicycle, or on foot; with new maps and location notes giving you the clearest directions possible.

The guide also contains the latest aerial photomaps to give you a much more accurate impression of our nature reserves than simple drawings. In addition to showing the size, shape and features of the reserves, these photomaps also highlight the fact that all too often they are islands of wildlife surrounded by a sea of intensively managed farmland, or housing or industrial developments.

We have worked with dedicated and knowledgeable local volunteers to ensure that all the wildlife information is as accurate as possible, and we have provided seasonal advice on each reserve, suggesting the best time to visit and some of the wildlife you may encounter when you are there.

The guide contains a stunning collection of wildlife and habitat photographs – many of them taken by Trust volunteers – which provide delightful records of the beauty of our nature reserves.

We hope that this book will help you to enjoy many wonderful days out in 'Wild Warwickshire', whether with family, friends or on your own. We also hope it will inspire you to visit more of these last remaining fragments of our natural heritage, as well as underlining the importance of protecting these places for generations to come.

Please contact Warwickshire Wildlife Trust if you would like further information on any of these nature reserves and the species found at them. The Trust's address is given on the cover. If you see any unusual occurrences, please also let us know. Finally, we value your feedback and would welcome any comments on this guide, or suggestions for future editions.

Brimstone butterfly

Wildlife habitats of Warwickshire, Coventry and Solihull

The natural habitats found at our nature reserves can be divided into four main groups, each of which provides vital sanctuaries for different species of wildlife:

- **Grassland –** from hay meadows to grazed pastures
- **Woodland** – including scrub and hedgerows
- **Wetland** – such as marshes, ponds, lakes and rivers
- **Artificial habitats** – from disused quarries to railway embankments

These areas and their distinctive wildlife are described more fully below.

GRASSLAND

Unlike the uniform bright green of heavily fertilised agricultural grassland, natural un-improved grassland tends to be tawny in colour, the result of a marvelous wealth of vibrantly coloured wildflowers growing amongst the many species of grasses. In prehistoric times, grasslands would have been maintained by herds of grazing animals from deer to bison, their constant chewing of the grass preventing trees from growing and enabling many wildflowers to thrive in the open conditions. These natural prairies and glades must have disappeared thousands of years ago, as our early ancestors tamed the wild beasts and agriculture developed. However, many of the plants have survived and still persist is small pockets today. In our area there are two main types of natural grassland, depending on the acidity or alkalinity of the underlying soil. Where grassland is grazed by cattle or sheep, it is usually known as a pasture, whereas if it is cut for hay then it is generally called a meadow.

Neutral pastures and meadows

Neutral pastures and meadows are found on soils that are neither strongly acidic nor strongly alkaline, and occur over most of central Warwickshire. Many show the 'ridge and furrow' pattern caused by medieval ploughing, as these fields used to be cultivated in the Middle Ages. Many reverted naturally to grassland after the Black Death in 1350 killed off 1/3rd of the population, leaving fewer people to plough the fields.

Once they became grassed over, centuries of traditional management by cutting hay every summer, before grazing the late growth (or 'aftermath') by cattle, has led to an amazing profusion of wild flowers. These in turn attract an array of insects – especially butterflies, grasshoppers and crickets – making old hay meadows a haven for wildlife. There are also ground-nesting birds such as skylark, and mammals such as moles, which thrive in this habitat.

The ancient ridge and furrow plough marks can still be seen at many of our grassland nature reserves, including **Draycote Meadows**, **Radway Meadows**, **Shadowbrook Meadows** and

Green-winged orchids

Swift Valley. Even **Brueton Park**, outside the Trust's Parkridge Centre in Solihull, still retains remnants of this ridge and furrow pattern, although the grassland here is mown short for its amenity value.

Looking more closely, the ridges and furrows in our nature reserves show strikingly different vegetation. Poorly drained areas at the bottom of the furrows support different wild flowers from the dry loving species thriving on the tops of the ridges. This gives rise to regular stripes of yellows and whites and greens across the meadows, from spring through to late summer.

Typical flowers of meadows include buttercups, cowslip, devil's-bit scabious, ragged-robin and oxeye daisy, with grasses such as sweet vernal-grass creating a special fragrance with every footstep. Less commonly, plants such as the delightful common spotted-orchid and adder's-tongue fern can be found.

May, June and early July are the months to view the meadows at their best. A host of birds including lapwing, corn bunting and meadow pipit may be seen, and the welcome song of the skylark can often be heard as it sings high above the meadow. Butterflies include the marbled white and meadow brown, with grasshoppers and crickets adding their typical summer sounds. You may be lucky to see a grass snake or slow-worm, basking in a more open area. Vole, shrew, mole, brown hare, badger, fox and bat make up the intricate assemblage of creatures that all rely on meadows for their survival.

In addition to the nature reserves listed above, **Brook Meadow**, **Deans Green**, **Harvest Hill**, **Loxley Church Meadow** and **Parliament Piece** are worthy of a visit to see this wonderful habitat, and **Alvecote Meadows** provides a wet meadow contrast. However if you only ever see one of these amazing fields, then **Draycote Meadows** is the place you should visit. There, every May, thousands of green-winged orchids join a medley of other wild flowers flourishing in the spring sunshine in a profusion not seen anywhere else in the Midlands.

Limestone and calcareous grassland

Breath-taking wild flowers can also be found growing on limestone or calcareous grassland. Developed on thin soils overlying limestone or lime-rich clays, these grasslands are awash with flowers during spring and summer. These sites are often associated with quarrying, and are found in the south and east of our county.

Looking unkempt in the winter, the seasons then give rise to distinct colour phases starting with yellow flowers in late spring turning to a profusion of pink, white, purples and blues in the summer, then oranges and browns in the autumn. These grasslands often display dozens of yellow meadow anthills, examples of which can be seen at **Welcombe Hills.**

Lapwing

The most stunning wildflower spectacles of limestone grassland are found on the old limestone quarry at **Ufton Fields**, and the discarded waste and exposed clays from cutting the railways in the mid-1800s at **Harbury Spoilbank** and **Stockton Cutting** nature reserves.

WOODLAND

After the last Ice Age some twelve thousand years ago, natural woodland developed over most of England. This 'wild wood' was a true wilderness and home to wolves, bears and wild boar. Today, only a tiny proportion of woodlands survive, but those that do provide living links with these ancient forests. Most of the Trust's woodland nature reserves are in this category of ancient woodland, and are older than our oldest cathedrals.

Ryton Wood

In addition to all the woodland cleared for agriculture or for urban developments, about half of our remaining woodland has been replaced with plantations of introduced conifers, which have little wildlife value. In total less than 3% of Warwickshire is now wooded, one of the lowest proportions in any county of England, making woodland one of our most important habitats.

The surviving ancient woods play host to distinctive plant and animal communities. Broad-leaved woodlands of oak and ash, found on heavy clay soils, give rise to swathes of bluebells and primroses. Wood anemone, dog's mercury, herb-Paris and yellow archangel are usually reliable indicators to the genuine ancient history of these woods, as they are very slow to colonise new woodland.

Butterflies thrive too, with uncommon white admiral and purple hairstreak as well as the more widespread speckled wood. But it is the woodland songbirds that provide the typical woodland experience for most people, with species including warblers and tits, nuthatch, treecreeper and greater spotted woodpecker.

Many of our woodland nature reserves are managed to maintain their diversity by coppicing, where branches are cut from a stump or 'stool' at ground level. Depending on the tree species and the number of years between coppicing, a variety of traditional woodland products can be made from the harvest including thatching spars, bean poles, hedge-laying materials and even charcoal.

Several species of tree will grow vigorously from the stool, particularly hazel and sweet chestnut. Within each area of coppice, a few trees (known as 'standards') are left uncut to grow to maturity, adding structure and variety to the woodland. During the period immediately after coppicing, more sunlight reaches the woodland floor. This gives rise to an explosion of colour on the ground with bluebell, primrose and wood anemone forming a carpet of flowers. As the young coppice shoots grow, they provide shelter and food for insects as well as excellent nesting sites for an array of woodland birds including nightingale.

Treecreeper

Excellent examples of coppiced woodland are found at **Hampton Wood**, **Ryton Wood** and **Snitterfield Bushes** with smaller areas at **Crackley Wood** and **Tocil Wood**, where volunteers have worked to reinstate coppice often neglected for decades. The impact of coppicing can be seen by comparing these woods with their uncoppiced cousins such as **Clowes Wood**, **Kenilworth Common**, **Rough Hill Wood** and **Wappenbury Wood**.

A distinctly different type of woodland can be found on seasonally or permanently waterlogged soil, known as wet woodland or 'carr'. Dominated by flood-resistant trees like willow and alder, these woods often occur in small patches next to other wetland habitats or in larger areas along rivers and marshes.

Hawthorn berries

The Trust manages a number of nature reserves where good examples of these wet woodlands are found, at sites such as **Stonebridge Meadows**, **Ufton Fields** and **Whitacre Heath**. These wet woods provide vital habitats for a range of insects and birds.

Scrub and hedgerows

Scrub develops where grassland is not managed by cutting or grazing, and species such as hawthorn and blackthorn invade to provide dense cover: ideal nesting places for many songbirds. If left unmanaged the natural process called succession will lead to other woody species like ash and eventually oak establishing, and after a few hundred years a mature woodland will develop.

Scrub is therefore a transitional habitat, managed by cutting to control its spread, with a constant dynamic between it and the surrounding grassland. Good examples can be found at **Ashlawn Cutting**, **Goldicote Cutting**, **Harbury Spoilbank** and **Knowle Hill**.

As woodland and tree cover have been significantly reduced over the centuries, hedgerows have become vital 'corridors' for species to travel between remaining patches of woodland. In Warwickshire there are two distinct types of hedge to be found in different parts of the county.

Hedges in the north and west – the area once known as 'Arden' – are very irregular, following the winding roads and paths of that part of the county. These hedges are often the last surviving remnants of ancient woodlands, host to many wild flowers and woody species like holly. In contrast hedges in south and east Warwickshire – once called the 'Feldon' – tend to be straight for hundreds of metres. This difference relates to the open field system of agriculture which once dominated the area, with few hedgerows and woodlands.

A hedges age can be estimated by the number and size of the trees found within them, with ancient hedgerows containing a much wider diversity of wildflower and tree species. In the Arden, look at the hedges around **Clowes Wood** or **Shadowbrook Meadows**, and compare them with the hedges of the Feldon near to **Ufton Fields** or **Tysoe Island**.

Wood white butterflies

WETLANDS

Brandon Marsh

The word wetland covers a wide variety of different habitats, united by the presence of water. Wetlands range from small ponds to large areas of marshy lakes, and also include all our rivers and streams. Our area spans the watershed of England, so that rain falling in North Warwickshire or Solihull will drain through the Rivers Blythe, Tame and Anker towards the Trent and the North Sea. Rain falling elsewhere flows through the Arrow, Leam and Avon to the Severn and then to the Irish Sea.

When the ice receded as the last Ice Age ended, melting glaciers would have provided Warwickshire with large areas of water in lakes, ponds, rivers and marshes. However these have long since disappeared and today there are no large natural lakes in our county, few marshes are left, and all the main rivers have been dredged. Even the water table itself has been lowered for the better existence of humans and their crops.

However, wetlands still thrive in our patch, thanks largely to our need for minerals like sand and gravel, which has led to extensive quarrying alongside all our main rivers. In addition to the rivers, streams and canals networks, there are also larger reservoirs at Draycote and Shustoke, smaller ponds in fields everywhere, and even garden ponds which provide a vital wildlife haven in towns and cities.

For ease of description, wetlands here are divided into two categories: marshland, and ponds and rivers.

Marshland

Marshes are themselves usually a patchwork of habitats, ranging from open water and reedbeds to wet woodland. This complexity contributes to a marvelous diversity of plants and animals which thrive in this type of habitat.

Typical plant species include yellow iris, flowering-rush, common bulrush and brooklime, amongst dozens of specialist water plants unable to survive in drier conditions. Waterlogged, dense vegetation, typical of marshland, provides important and vital habitat for nesting birds such as water rail, warblers, snipe and bittern. Good examples of marsh habitat can be found at **Brandon Marsh** and the nearby **Claybrookes Marsh** on the edge of Coventry, **Ufton Fields**, and **Whitacre Heath** on the River Tame. Smaller areas of marsh can be found at **Pooley Fields** and **Eathorpe Marsh**.

Yellow iris

Ponds and rivers

The open water of ponds and rivers supports whole ecosystems of life, from microscopic algae through a multitude of invertebrates like water boatmen and dragonfly nymphs to great crested newts, fish, water vole and even otter. The size of the water body and its speed of flow are critical in determining which species can survive where, some preferring the still waters of ponds, others fast-flowing streams.

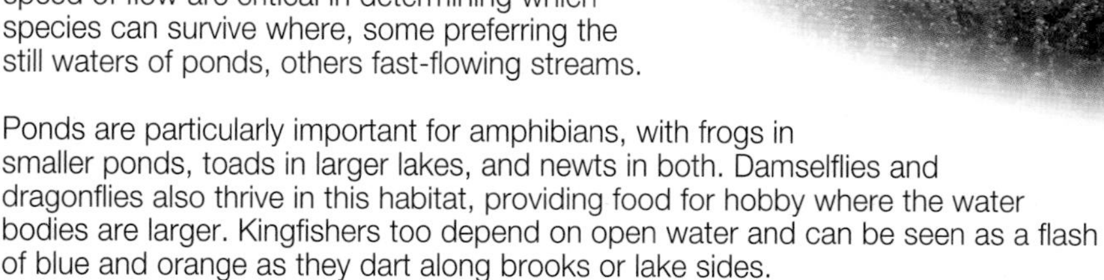

Stoke Floods

Ponds are particularly important for amphibians, with frogs in smaller ponds, toads in larger lakes, and newts in both. Damselflies and dragonflies also thrive in this habitat, providing food for hobby where the water bodies are larger. Kingfishers too depend on open water and can be seen as a flash of blue and orange as they dart along brooks or lake sides.

Large areas of open water are the main attractions for wildlife and for people at **Pooley Fields**, **Stoke Floods** and **Wyken Slough**, the latter two linking with **Stonebridge Meadows** along the Sowe Valley, a green corridor sweeping though the east side of Coventry. Smaller pools are found in many nature reserves, including **Parliament Piece** in Kenilworth, **Cock Robin Wood** in Rugby and **Elmdon Manor** in Solihull.

Although none of our rivers are Trust nature reserves, the River Blythe in Solihull is designated as an SSSI – one of the few rivers in England to be protected in this way. Rivers form the boundary of several nature reserves, with the River Avon linking **Brandon Marsh** near Coventry with **Hampton Wood** south of Warwick and **Cox's Island** in Stratford-upon-Avon. Other riverside reserves include the **Leam Valley**, **Welches Meadow** and **Whitnash Brook** in Leamington Spa and the **River Arrow** in Alcester. Many of these sites also feature 'pollarded' willows. Pollarding was a traditional way of managing willow by cutting them off about two metres above the ground, then letting the mass of shoots grow for a few years, before they were harvested for fencing, thatching and any of the other uses for the thin flexible stems. Nowadays there is little commercial market, but pollarding is continued to help stabilise river banks and provide vital nesting sites for birds and shelter for many insects.

Kingfisher

Stockton Cutting

ARTIFICIAL HABITATS

All of our nature reserves have been influenced in some ways by people, whether by the cutting of grass in meadows, or the coppicing of woodland. However, the history of Warwickshire since the industrial revolution has left a legacy of sites that were once thriving industrial areas, then derelict eyesores and now have been reclaimed by nature.

Coal mining was the industrial foundation at **Pooley Fields**, and subsidence from Binley Colliery created the wetland at **Stoke Floods**, the landscape of **Claybrookes Marsh**, and the first subsidence pools at **Brandon Marsh**.

Quarrying for sand and gravel created the larger pools at **Brandon Marsh** in the Avon valley and at **Whitacre Heath** in the Tame valley, where some excavations were later filled with fly-ash waste. Quarrying for limestone was the creative force at the nature reserves of **Newbold Quarry** and **Ufton Fields**. In addition to these Trust reserves there are many other important wildlife sites in disused quarries throughout our area.

The construction of the railways must have blighted the landscape of Warwickshire in the mid-1800s, but now the naturally colonised cuttings and embankments have developed into tranquil nature reserves at **Ashlawn Cutting**, **Goldicote Cutting**, **Harbury Spoilbank**, **Henley Sidings** and **Stockton Cutting**. Canals too now provide quiet links for nature where once industrial uses reigned.

Currently the only reserve created by design rather than by accident is **Cock Robin Wood** near Rugby, which was planted on a barley field in the 1980s as part of the planning conditions for the nearby Sainsbury's supermarket. However, as we look to the future, there is a growing need to link up natural places and restore large areas for wildlife – so Cock Robin Wood is unlikely to be the only created reserve for long.

There are two other categories of artificial habitats that have some value for wildlife: agricultural land and gardens. Farming is the biggest use of the land across our area, and although many of the fields have little wildlife value due to the intensive way that they are farmed, the hedgerows and spinneys, copses, ponds and streams provide vital links, joining up the more important habitats. Domestic gardens also have significant value, providing a network of trees and shrubs, garden ponds and small wildlife areas dotted throughout the urban environment.

Our nature reserves

Many of Warwickshire Wildlife Trust's nature reserves are owned by the Trust, but others are owned by various partners – mainly local authorities – and managed through leases or agreements with the owners. We are very grateful for the support of all these partners, who are listed in full at the end of the book.

Some of our nature reserves are protected through national legislation. SSSI (or Site of Special Scientific Interest) is a designation given to the top wildlife sites in the country by Natural England, the government's conservation advisors. The only category above this is NNR (National Nature Reserve) but there are none of these in our area. LNR (or Local Nature Reserve) is the category below SSSI, which provides good accessibility as well as good habitats for wildlife. Where our nature reserves have these designations, you will find them listed in the detailed pages that follow.

All our nature reserves are managed for wildlife and for people through management plans, which take into account the complex of factors, both natural and man-made, that can improve or detract from the site's value. Once a management plan has been agreed between all the key people, it is up to The Trust's staff and volunteers, working closely together, to carry out the necessary work. There is more information about volunteering on page 117.

Landscape-scale conservation

Traditionally, nature conservation in Britain has focused on protecting areas of land as nature reserves. This action aimed to safeguard key areas, but it didn't prevent other changes in the landscape, such as the loss of 40% of reedbeds since 1945 and 97% of species-rich grasslands since the 1930s. Nature reserves are now like small islands in a sea of intensive farmland, housing and industry. As climate change impacts become more real, the need to do something more than just protecting these small areas becomes all the more clear.

Alvecote Pools SSSI

In fact wildlife itself has been detecting our changing climate for the last twenty years or more, with many species moving further north. Cetti's warbler, a Mediterranean species, was a rare bird in the south-east of England in the early 1970s. It reached Brandon Marsh, its most northerly site in Britain, in 1994. Now several pairs breed regularly at Brandon, and its northern limit has passed the Wirral in Cheshire.

Cetti's warbler is not just an isolated example. A recent national study showed that 80% of the 300 species investigated had moved between 30 and 60 km further north in the last 25 years alone. And those species that can't move – the plants – are now flowering earlier than ever before, with snowdrops now flowering on average three weeks earlier than in the 1980s.

Faced with these challenges, The Wildlife Trusts and others have been working to develop solutions to provide a positive future for wildlife within these islands. Under the heading of 'Living Landscapes', Wildlife Trusts are working with farmers and landowners, with other charities, Government agencies and local councils, to link together fragmented nature reserves and other wildlife sites, creating large areas for wildlife, linked by new natural networks.

In Warwickshire we have made an excellent start, thanks to a county-wide audit of our natural heritage completed in the year 2000 by the Trust in partnership with all our local councils, Natural England and the Environment Agency. This Habitat Biodiversity Audit was based on aerial photographs and field-by-field surveys, and shows the wildlife value of every single part of our patch on a computer-based mapping system.

Ryton Woods

From this Millennium Map some parts of the county stand out as beacons with high wildlife value, and by developing these areas for targeted natural restoration, the resulting large areas will have benefits for wildlife much greater than the sum of their parts. In addition, by linking existing sites together a new ecological network can be developed, providing long-term security for wildlife.

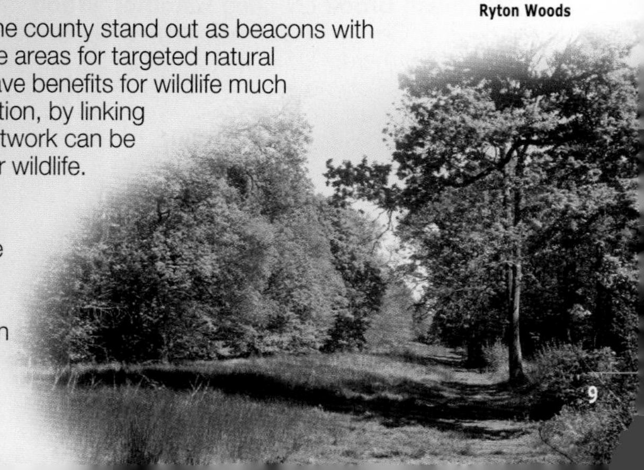

Tame valley wetlands

Heading northwards from the River Blythe SSSI into Staffordshire, the Tame valley links many existing wetlands, including **Whitacre Heath** SSSI, RSPB's Middleton Hall and the County Council's Kingsbury

Water Park as well as **Alvecote Meadows** SSSI and **Pooley Fields** SSSI on the River Anker. By working with other landowners we hope to create new wetlands and restore the natural floodplains, adding to wildlife, flood defence measures and the potential for greater green tourism.

Princethorpe woodlands

Within 5 km to the south of Coventry, a cluster of 16 woodlands around Princethorpe forms the largest and most important area of ancient woodlands in the county, covering over four hundred hectares and including **Ryton Wood** SSSI, **Wappenbury Wood** and **Old Nun Wood**. Reconnecting these woodlands through sympathetic land management and woodland creation will encourage wildlife with additional gains for sustainable woodland management.

Brandon Marsh area

Brandon Marsh SSSI is part of the River Avon corridor, and also links to other sites including **Claybrookes Marsh** SSSI, the Woodland Trust's Piles Coppice, Brandon Wood and Coombe Abbey Country Park. With a range of different habitats, this area has the potential to become a natural landscape of regional importance for wildlife and informal recreation.

Southam grasslands

The area around Southam is home to a group of old quarry workings and railway cuttings, now nature reserves such as **Harbury Spoilbank** SSSI, **Ufton Fields** SSSI and **Stockton Cutting** SSSI. By enhancing these areas and creating new links between them, many uncommon species will benefit.

Forest of Arden

On the western side of the county lies the historic Forest of Arden landscape – a mosaic of ancient small fields and woods including Trust nature reserves at **Brook Meadow** SSSI, **Clowes Wood** SSSI, **Deans Green**, **Shadowbrook Meadows** SSSI, **Temple Balsall** and the smaller **Earlswood Moathouse** and **Henley Sidings**. The aim here is to retain the old pastures and woodlands, to attract more wildlife to this special historic landscape.

Cotswolds and Edge Hill

The scarp slope of Edge Hill links the south-east of the county to the Cotswolds Area of Outstanding Natural Beauty in Oxfordshire and Gloucestershire. Enhancing links between nature reserves including **Radway Meadows** and the tiny **Tysoe Island** will encourage farmland birds and grassland butterflies.

Severn and Avon Vale

The River Avon, with its tributaries and surrounding floodplains, contributes to a valuable wetland wildlife corridor including **Eathorpe Marsh**, **Leam Valley** LNR, **Welches Meadow** LNR, **Whitnash Brook** LNR and **Hampton Wood** nature reserves. Linking to other wetlands along the River Severn in Worcestershire and Gloucestershire, there is huge potential for large-scale restoration here.

Visiting Trust Nature Reserves

Have a safe visit

We want to make sure that you have a safe and enjoyable time when visiting our nature reserves. We take every care to ensure that our reserves are as safe as possible, but you should remember that they are natural places, with natural hazards. Help yourself on your visit by:

- wearing strong shoes or boots and appropriate clothing for the weather conditions
- letting someone know where you are going and when you expect to return
- bringing this guide with you, as not all our reserves have signs to guide you
- always taking notice of danger warning signs
- being aware of potential hazards such as deep water, steep slopes or falling rocks
- keeping to marked paths at all times
- staying away from rivers and flooded fields after heavy rain

If you need any further information about safety on our nature reserves, contact our offices (address on cover).

How you can help

Trust staff and volunteers regularly check paths, steps and bridges for damage but should you come across any damage, vandalism or inappropriate behaviour when visiting our reserves, please contact us immediately (contact details on cover).

Dogs cause disturbance and distress to both wildlife and livestock. Visitors with dogs should keep them under control and on leads at all times. On some of our sensitive reserves, dogs are not permitted, even on leads, so please check the 'Getting Around' section of each nature reserve description to find this information. Please also clear up your dog's mess.

You can help us to conserve the special character of our nature reserves by keeping to the paths and always taking your litter home. Don't start any fires, especially in summer months, and don't take away any plants, animals or fossils. But do enjoy the peace, tranquillity and wildlife, and let us know of any sightings that you think are important.

Always remember: Take only photographs, leave only footprints, kill only time.

Thank you.

How to use this book

This Guide has been produced to make it as easy as possible for you to visit our nature reserves.

If you want to visit a nature reserve near your home, you can refer to the map on the inside front cover, which lists all our reserves by name and location in the county, along with their page numbers. If you already know the name of the reserve you wish to visit, you can refer to the index on page 124, which will take you to the site entry.

We have also grouped our reserves together depending on their size and ecological importance. Our larger, more special reserves are marked with a green 'traffic light' symbol, our medium reserves with an amber light and our smaller reserves with a red light. Each reserve is listed alphabetically in its colour coded section.

GETTING THERE

This includes a road map and location notes, the sheet number for the 1:50,000 Ordinance Survey Landranger Map, plus the Grid Reference for the main entrance to the reserve. Information is also given on parking and public transport.

GETTING AROUND

This should help you decide whether the site is suitable before you visit. It gives the size of the reserve, description of the terrain, path conditions and any obstacles you may encounter.

Dogs are permitted on many sites and MUST be kept on short leads at all times. On some of the more sensitive sites dogs are not allowed.

BEST TIME TO VISIT

The pop-up tabs indicate the best time to visit the reserve and some of the wildlife you may encounter. Some reserves may be at their best for short periods of the year, and for these reserves, only the relevant seasons are displayed.

Great spotted woodpecker

Bluebell and orange-tip butterfly

STATUS

The traffic light symbols provide an indication of the general appeal of the reserve. It reflects how easy it is to get around the site and the variety of interest there. It does not reflect the value of the site to wildlife or people!

Green light – These sites are considered well worth the travelling time to visit, even if you don't live locally. 'Green' sites tend to have several of the following attributes: good access, parking, waymarked wildlife walks, hides, scenic landscape, large size, sufficient interest to warrant a longer visit.

Amber light – Worth a visit for a shorter period of time. The sites may have several of the qualities found at 'green' sites but may be smaller in size and hold less interest. Worth regular visits if nearby.

Red light – Worth a visit if you live locally. These sites tend to be small and lack most of the qualities of 'green' and 'amber' sites. They are nevertheless important for conservation.

SSSI – Site of Special Scientific Interest – see box, page 8.

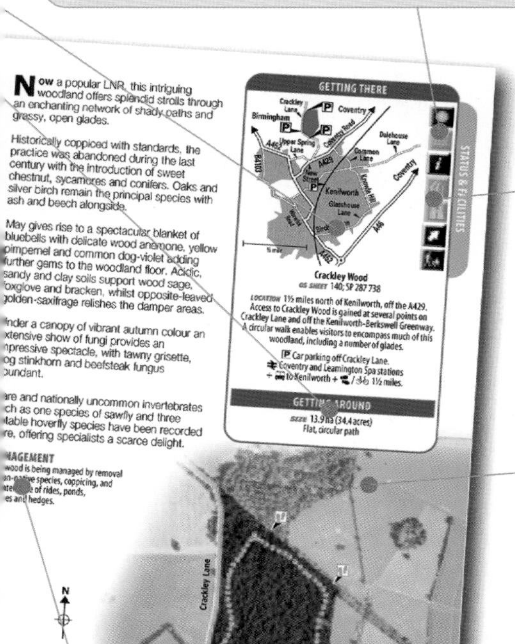

Now a popular LNR, this intriguing woodland offers splendid strolls through an enchanting network of shady paths and grassy, open glades.

Historically coppiced with standards, the practice was abandoned during the last century with the introduction of sweet chestnut, sycamores and conifers. Oaks and silver birch remain the principal species with ash and beech alongside.

May gives rise to a spectacular blanket of bluebells with delicate wood anemone, yellow pimpernel and common dog-violet adding further gems to the woodland floor. Acidic, sandy and clay soils support wood sage, foxglove and bracken, whilst opposite-leaved golden-saxifrage relishes the damper areas.

Under a canopy of vibrant autumn colour an extensive show of fungi provides an impressive spectacle, with tawny grisette, dog stinkhorn and beefsteak fungus abundant.

Rare and nationally uncommon invertebrates such as one species of sawfly and three notable hoverfly species have been recorded here, offering specialists a scarce delight.

MANAGEMENT

The wood is being managed by removal of non-native species, coppicing, and maintenance of rides, ponds, ditches and hedges.

GETTING THERE

Crackley Wood

OS SHEET 140; SP 287 738

LOCATION 1½ miles north of Kenilworth, off the A429. Access to Crackley Wood is gained at several points on Crackley Lane and off the Kenilworth-Berkswell Greenway. A circular walk enables visitors to encompass much of this woodland, including a number of glades.

Car parking off Crackley Lane.

Coventry and Leamington Spa stations to Kenilworth 1½ miles.

GETTING AROUND

SIZE 13.9 ha (34.4 acres)

Flat, circular path

STATUS & FACILITIES

FACILITIES

Information panels

Visitor Centre

Hides to watch wildlife

Marked nature trails

Access for people with limited mobility

RESERVE MAP

All reserve maps are orientated north, with a scale of 1 cm to 100 m

The key to paths and map symbols is shown here and also on the flaps of the cover, which enables you to use the key whilst viewing the map.

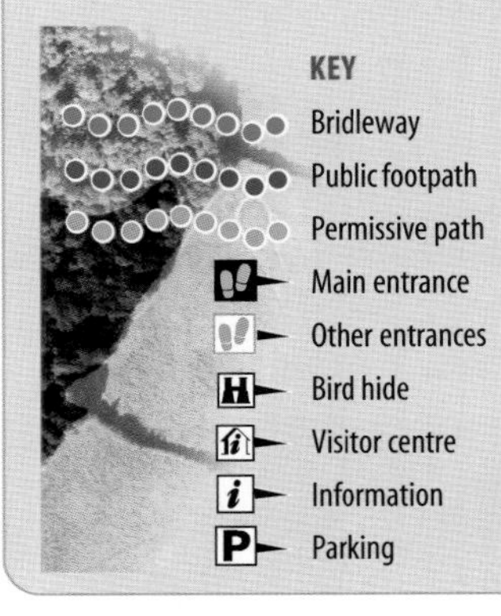

MANAGEMENT

Most of our reserves are actively managed to ensure they maintain their conservation value. This section gives a brief insight into the kind of work we carry out at each reserve.

Water rail

Brandon Marsh

This magnificent wetland SSSI, with its patchwork of pools, marsh, reedbed, grassland and woodland, is one of the jewels in the crown of the Trust's nature reserves

Best time to visit

WINTER ✔

BIRDS Teal (BELOW), pochard, shoveler, geese, grebes, kingfisher, bittern, siskin

SPRING ✔

PLANTS Red campion
AMPHIBIANS Newts
BIRDS Waders, great crested grebe (BELOW), common tern, skylark, reed warbler, Cetti's warbler, water rail

SUMMER ✔

PLANTS Southern marsh- and common spotted-orchids
INSECTS Four-spotted chaser (BELOW) and other dragonflies, damselflies, water boatman, whirlygig beetle
BIRDS Hobby
MAMMALS Badger, bats

AUTUMN ✔

FUNGI Jellybabies (BELOW), waxcaps
BIRDS Lapwing, green sandpiper

Home to the Trust's headquarters since 1992, this premier reserve boasts a thriving Visitor and Education Centre, conference facilities, picturesque tearoom and a delightful gift shop.

Lying south-east of the busy city of Coventry and flanked by a meandering stretch of the River Avon, Brandon Marsh SSSI offers tranquil walks amongst a mosaic of habitats. An extensive network of paths and a marked nature trail provide the opportunity to explore the reserve and experience its wide range of wildlife.

Well over 230 bird species have been recorded, 60 of which choose the site to breed, annually. The reserve's seven bird hides provide fantastic sightings of ducks, geese, waders and other wetland birds that flock to the site. Teal, shoveler and pochard vie for attention with grebes, sandpipers, kingfisher, and even snipe and water rail.

Raptors are frequent, with regular sightings of kestrel, sparrowhawk, buzzard, hobby and occasional harriers. With its deserved reputation for attracting rare birds on migration, the Brandon Marsh 'sightings board' often boasts osprey and long-eared owl.

With the largest reedbed in Warwickshire, the site has successfully attracted, and celebrated, the arrival of many rare species, including bittern, a 'red alert' bird, and the captivating otter.

With some 500 plants recorded, the reserve's rich flora offers a multiplicity of splendors, from bulrush fringing the open waters, to lovely southern marsh- and common spotted-orchids.

The two small woodlands are over 200 years old and include many tree species such as oak, ash and hazel. Hope Wood at the centre of the reserve was planted as a memorial wood. A beautiful area in which to reflect, it now provides rich fruit pickings for birds under its colourful autumn canopy.

... continued overleaf ▶

Reed warbler

Amphibians flourish at Brandon Marsh, including great crested, palmate and smooth newts. Pond dipping opportunities probe the aquatic world of water boatman, whirligig beetle and pond snails. Alien-like dragonfly larvae are commonly netted, eventually destined to fly the summer skies as adult dragonflies and damselflies.

Areas of undisturbed grassland and brambles attract butterflies, with a dozen or so species expected on a summer visit. The squeaks and disputes of common shrew and field vole may be heard amongst the long grass where fox, stoat and wily weasel hunt the prolific rabbit population.

Muntjac deer hide in the reedbeds and woodland undergrowth where signs of badger activity may be seen. Bats are plentiful, attracted by the rich insect pickings, and during the evenings may be seen as they dart low over the pools.

A final richness is found in the reserve's extensive fungi list, with up to 600 species identified from field birdsnest in the sensory garden, to waxcaps in the short grass and jellybabies hiding in the woods!

Brandon Fields, to the north of Brandon Lane, provides public footpath links to the nearby Brandon Wood and Piles Coppice, and to Claybrookes Marsh SSSI beyond the A46.

MANAGEMENT

Wetland
Removal of invasive willow from reedbeds and marsh.
Reed planting within newly created wetland areas.
Islands and some marsh areas strimmed in late summer.

Wet woodland
Thinning of willows to increase light to ground flora and improve structural diversity.

Dry woodland
Thinning of oak standards and understorey planting with hazel.

Grassland
Grass is cut for hay by a local farmer.

Paths and hides
Path edges cut regularly to ensure they are accessible.
Hides and interpretation boards kept in good repair.
Bird and bat boxes monitored regularly.

GETTING THERE

Brandon Marsh

OS SHEET 140; SP 386 761

LOCATION 3 miles south-east of Coventry. The reserve is situated on Brandon Lane which can be accessed off the A45 or through Brandon Village.

P Large surfaced car park at reserve
Rugby or Coventry + bus to Brandon village + walk / cycle 1½ miles; or bus to Willenhall + walk / cycle 2 miles; or bus to Wolston + walk / cycle 1½ miles.

GETTING AROUND

SIZE 92.3 ha (228 acres)
There are a number of well surfaced, way-marked paths which intersect the site. Relatively flat, wheelchair friendly. Stretches prone to flooding and mud in winter
No dogs allowed on this reserve except for guide dogs

Shaggy scalycap

Clowes Wood and New Fallings Coppice

This substantial ancient woodland SSSI has a fascinating mosaic of trees and shrubs, ditches, streams, pond, small reclaimed meadow and a precious remnant heathland

Best time to visit

SPRING ✔

PLANTS Lily-of-the-valley, sanicle, marsh-marigold, wood anemone, wood-sorrel, wood spurge, bluebell, marsh violet, bilberry (BELOW)
BIRDS Woodpeckers, tawny owl
MAMMALS Muntjac deer signs

SUMMER ✔

PLANTS Heath spotted-orchid, lemon-scented fern, heather, wood sage, common cow-wheat, sneezewort (BELOW), wood horsetail
INSECTS Brimsone and speckled wood butterflies

AUTUMN ✔

FUNGI Red-cracking bolete, blusher, shaggy scalycap
PLANTS Beech leaf colour, bilberry fruit, lily-of-the-valley fruit (BELOW)

WINTER ✔

FUNGI Scarlet elfcup
BIRDS Woodcock (BELOW)

Clowes Wood was the first reserve owned by the Trust – acquired in 1975 by the generosity of an anonymous donor.

From 1908 the Birmingham to Stratford railway bisected the forest into Big Clowes to the south and Little Clowes and New Fallings Coppice to the north. The area has probably been wooded since the last ice age, despite being almost clear-felled in the early 1900s, and indeed a 'closed' wood was chronicled here in the late 13th century. The wood's name probably derives from the Latin 'Clausus' or French 'Clos' referring to enclosure.

Offering some archaeological interest, a burnt stone pile on the site dates back 4,000 years to the Bronze Age and may have been used for a sweat lodge or sauna.

The woodlands stand mostly on acidic gravels and contain both penduculate and sessile oak, plus silver and downy birch. Holly, aspen and rowan are frequent, whilst areas of impeded drainage welcome alder and willow. The mixture is enriched further with a medley of other species, including the rare wild service-tree, and a large stand of beech increases biodiversity and provides spectacular colour changes in the autumn.

Bluebells, wood-sorrel and wood anemone herald the arrival of spring, along with less common ramsons and other woodland flowers such as wood spurge and lily-of-the-valley.

Once nearly overwhelmed by aspen and scrub, the wet meadow is now species-rich grassland once again, and plants include heath spotted-orchid and marsh violet, and most recently, lemon-scented fern. Damper parts show rushes and sedges, and in the adjoining marshy woodland, marsh-marigold and wood horsetail prosper.

... continued overleaf ▶

Wood anemones

The small heathy area presents heather, bilberry, wood sage, purple moor-grass and bracken. A wealth of fungi appears both under and on the varied trees, from red-cracking bolete and blusher to shaggy scalycap and scarlet elfcup. Slime moulds add an intriguing feature and perhaps may even tempt a new interest for some.

Fifty species of bird breed here such as jay, chiffchaff, nuthatch and treecreeper, with tawny owl, woodcock and lesser spotted woodpecker adding some rarities to the list. Further surveys have produced long lists of insects, identifying a number of scarce flies, bees, wasps and beetles. Indeed, Clowes Wood is the richest woodland in the north-west of the county for macromoths, including the very local light orange underwing.

Badger activity is evident in this woodland and red fox, muntjac and brown hare are all regular visitors to this reserve.

GETTING THERE

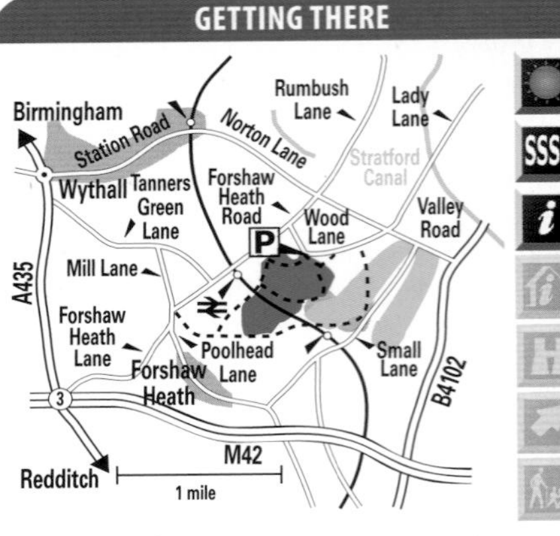

STATUS & FACILITIES

SSSI

Clowes Wood and New Fallings Coppice

OS SHEET 139; SP 101 743

LOCATION Situated 5 miles south of Solihull, access point on Wood Lane.

P Car park on Wood Lane.

Earlswood + / ½ mile.

GETTING AROUND

SIZE 44.5 ha (110 acres)
Gently sloping, extensive path network, some areas prone to becoming muddy, narrow bridges and steps

MANAGEMENT

Woodland
Thinning of oak standards and removal of invasive holly to encourage natural regeneration and increase structural diversity.

Wet woodland
Removal of invasive non-native Himalayan balsam by hand pulling.

Wet meadow
Grassland sward cut in late summer / early autumn and the cuttings removed.

Heathland
Removal of encroaching scrub to maintain the area of heath.

Paths
Regular maintenance of paths as they have a tendency to get very wet.

Jay

Green-winged orchid

Draycote Meadows

These picturesque, traditional hay meadows are the 'crème de la crème' of remaining unimproved grassland found in Warwickshire today. Bounded by old hedgerows and a stream, these species-rich meadows support a tremendous diversity of plants and animals, and could not be more worthy of their SSSI status

Best time to visit

SPRING ✔

PLANTS Cowslip (BELOW), green-winged orchid, twayblade, buttercups, adder's-tongue, moonwort, grasses
BIRDS Woodpeckers, nuthatch
INSECTS Small copper and orange-tip butterflies

SUMMER ✔

PLANTS Meadow vetchling, lesser water-parsnip, brooklime, knapweed, common spotted-orchid, bee orchid
INSECTS Common blue (BELOW) and marbled white butterflies

AUTUMN ✔

FUNGI Waxcaps, meadow coral, smokey spindles, white spindles (BELOW)

WINTER

Lying over neutral, heavy, lias clay soils, the meadows offer a fine example of ridge and furrow, hinting that these grasslands have ancient origins. Both meadows are managed traditionally as hay meadows, with their crops cut in late July and the aftermath grazed by cattle in the autumn.

The grassland presents waves of buttercup, cowslip, meadow vetchling and yellow rattle. Twenty species of grass complete the mass to form seas of tawny green with bursts of colour. In addition to its many grasses, the southern meadow offers a wide range of plants including the inconspicuous adder's-tongue fern. Even rare moonwort is recorded in this meadow, its only known location in Warwickshire. Both meadows are renowned for spectacular displays of green-winged orchid, indicating the undisturbed antiquity of the site. Thousands of flower spikes, in an array of colour forms, enchant visitors every year.

Butterflies are abundant, with small copper and common blue dancing across the meadows and along the hedgerows.

An autumn visit can produce an amazing list of fungi, with an impressive dozen species of waxcap alone. Other distinctive fungi include white and smokey spindles and meadow coral.

The stream, with its spring-fed waters supports brooklime, lesser water-parsnip and meadowsweet which grow on its margins.

The hedgerows contain English elm, blackthorn and wild privet mingled with ivy and dog-rose. Occasional specimens of oak, ash and wild cherry add further diversity to the hedge line.

A good range of birds nest and roost in the trees and hedgerow, including nuthatch, great spotted and green woodpeckers. Redwing and fieldfare relish the reserve in winter months.

MANAGEMENT

An annual hay crop is cut and removed each year by a local farmer. The later growth (or 'aftermath') is grazed by cattle.

GETTING THERE

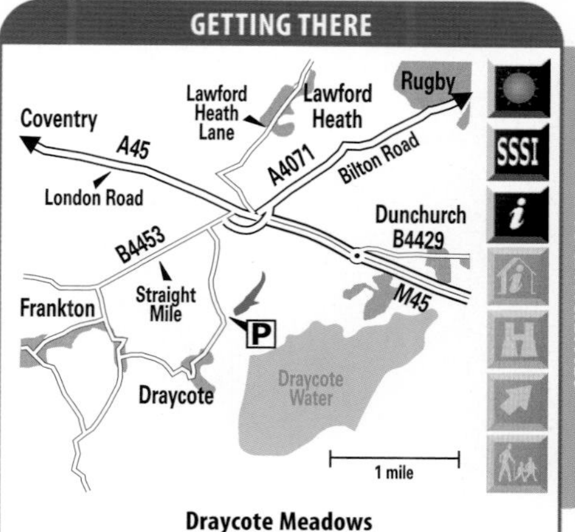

Draycote Meadows
OS SHEET 140; SP 448 706

LOCATION 4 miles south-west of Rugby, just north of Draycote Village. Turn off the B4453 near to the A45 London Road interchange, the reserve is approx ½ mile along the lane.

P Parking at reserve entrance.
Rugby + bus to Draycote + walk / cycle (footpaths) ½ mile.

GETTING AROUND

SIZE 5.5 ha (13.6 acres)
No defined paths, please keep to boundaries. Access to the northern meadow is restricted to organised events which are included in the Trust's summer events programme.
No dogs allowed on this reserve

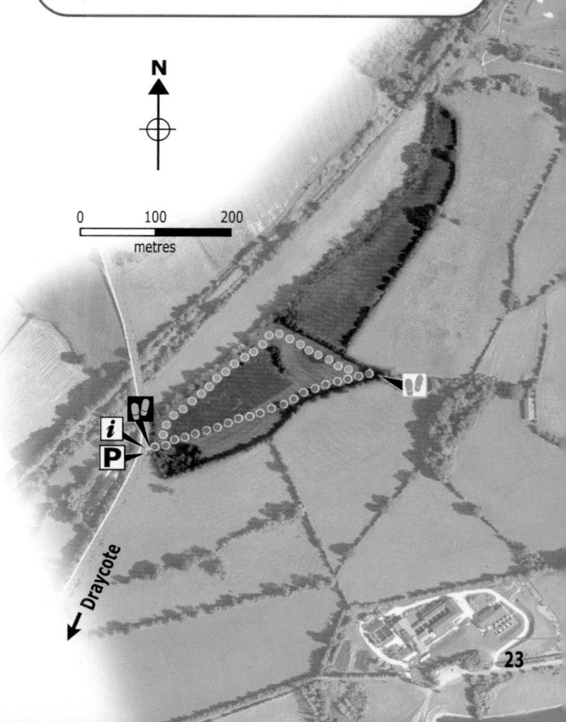

Wavy bladderwort

Pooley Fields

An impressive mosaic of pools, swamp, marsh, woodland and grassy areas makes this scenic reserve an oasis for marsh-loving plants, amphibians and wetland birds

Best time to visit

WINTER ✔

BIRDS Linnet (BELOW), reed bunting, finches, pied wagtail, great crested grebe

SPRING ✔

PLANTS Yellow iris (BELOW), tormentil, bird's-foot-trefoil
INSECTS Dingy skipper butterfly
AMPHIBIANS Frog, toad, great crested newt
REPTILES Grass snake
BIRDS Swallow, reed bunting, sedge warbler

SUMMER ✔

PLANTS Wavy bladderwort, hemlock water-dropwort, southern marsh-orchid, blue fleabane, sand spurrey
INSECTS Dragonflies, including hairy dragonfly (BELOW), damselflies, purple hairstreak butterfly, elephant hawkmoth, long-horned dancing moth

AUTUMN ✔

FUNGI Fly agaric (BELOW), brittlegills, earthball
PLANTS Birch leaf colour
BIRDS Linnet and other finches

Together with neighbouring Alvecote Meadows reserve, Pooley Fields forms Warwickshire's largest SSSI, Alvecote Pools.

Once the location of Pooley Hall Colliery, coal was mined at the site between 1848 and 1965. Subsidence and flooding later created today's complex of habitats, with their considerable diversity.

Common reed and bulrush fringe the pools with many other wetland plants including sedges, yellow iris and water figwort. The open water supports water-lilies, pondweeds, water-crowfoot and duckweed. Rare insectivorous wavy bladderwort lurks below the surface, its only location in Warwickshire.

Swamp with greater pond-sedge grades into marsh, with flowers such as hemlock water-dropwort and a colony of southern marsh-orchid. Willow and alder grow here, with sphagnum moss in some places. Common frog and toad, along with smooth and great crested newt, all relish these damp spots, which also provide excellent hunting grounds for grass snake.

The woodland is dominated by stunted oak and silver birch, which display rich carpets of moss and lichen on their branches. Bracken also thrives, giving rise to rich colour later in the year. A substantial range of fungi appears in autumn including earthball, brittlegills and fly agaric.

Grassy clearings contain pleasant flowers such as bird's-foot trefoil, tormentil and goat's-beard. Drier areas have blue fleabane and even sand spurrey.

Insects are well represented and lists are extensive. Twenty-one species of dragonfly provide regular viewings of hawkers, chasers and darters whilst diminutive little damselflies are numerous. Scores of butterflies are noted, including purple hairstreak and dingy skipper.

... continued overleaf ▶

Hemlock water-dropwort

The impressive elephant hawkmoth larvae can also be found, as can six-belted clearwing and long-horned dancing moth. More specialist invertebrates recorded include 28 species that are nationally rare.

Birds are countless, using the reserve to feed, nest and roost; and include great crested grebe, reed bunting, sedge warbler, pied wagtail and flocks of linnets and other finches. Swallows frequent the reserve, skimming low over the pools for insects, performing impressive displays of aerial acrobatics.

A large spoilheap lies outside the reserve and SSSI, but it offers panoramic views over the site, making it well worthy of the climb. Coventry Canal defines the western boundary of the reserve and offers further opportunities for splendid walks.

MANAGEMENT

Wetland
Removal of invasive willow from reedbed fringes and marsh to open up edges of pools. Rotational removal of silt from pools to ensure they continue to hold water all year round.

Wet woodland
Thinning and pollarding of willows to increase light to ground flora and improve structural diversity.

Woodland glades
Cut annually.

Common frog

Elephant hawkmoth

GETTING THERE

Pooley Fields

OS SHEET 138; SK 244 048

LOCATION Between Polesworth and Tamworth in north Warwickshire. Access to the site off Robeys Lane.

P Limited parking at entrance off Robeys Lane. Car park at Pooley Heritage Centre (charge applicable).

Tamworth + No. 785 to Alvecote + / ½ mile.

GETTING AROUND

SIZE 26.2 ha (64.7 acres)

Flat, wheel chair access adjacent to canal, kissing gates, muddy in winter

Reed bunting

Silver-washed fritillary

Ryton Wood

This ancient wood is one of eight large woods, which together form the Princethorpe Woodlands – these vital woods are the largest surviving area of semi-natural woodland left in Warwickshire today

Best time to visit

WINTER ✔

PLANTS Small-leaved lime stools, field maple, guelder-rose
MAMMALS Muntjac (BELOW)

SPRING ✔

PLANTS Bluebell, primrose, wood anemone, yellow pimpernel (BELOW), barren strawberry, yellow archangel
AMPHIBIANS Smooth newt, common frog, toad
REPTILES Grass snake
BIRDS Woodpeckers, cuckoo, little owl, song birds
MAMMALS Badger, fox, stoat, weasel

SUMMER ✔

PLANTS Common spotted-orchid, broad-leaved helleborine, devil's-bit scabious, honeysuckle
INSECTS White admiral, silver-washed fritillary, wood white and purple hairstreak butterflies, damselflies, ruddy darter (BELOW) and other dragonflies, beetles
BIRDS Buzzard, sparrowhawk

AUTUMN ✔

FUNGI Parasitic bolete and earthball (BELOW), collared earthstar, silky piggyback

Although part of Ryton Wood was lost to sand and gravel extraction in the 1960s, the wood has been returned to its present excellence though traditional management practices.

Arguably the best of the Princethorpe Woods, Ryton Wood covers an extensive 85 hectares and indeed is the only one to have been designated as an SSSI, boasting an extensive list of notable species.

Parts of this outstanding reserve are historically confirmed as 11th century, almost certainly implying the land has been wooded since the last ice age relented. The existence of coppiced small-leaved lime stools provides evidence to support this. Once the most common tree 5,000 years ago, the species is now very infrequent. Huge ditches also indicate the wood's ancient, medieval boundaries.

Forty or so species of tree and shrub have been identified, with oak dominant. Hazel forms the principal understorey, where an abundance of honeysuckle, our county flower, scrambles through, sweetening the air on summer days.

Joyfully celebrating spring, primrose, wood anemone and yellow pimpernel carpet the woodland floor. The radiating rides are grassy and bright and the extra light permits a further range of plants to colonise, such as barren strawberry and common spotted-orchid. Broad-leaved helleborine favours the dappled edges of the rides. Some of the large, clear glades give rise to fabulous bluebell displays and dense stands of bracken.

With its medley of habitats, Ryton Wood boasts a substantial list of insects and is the best site for butterflies in Warwickshire. Species to be seen include white admiral, purple hairstreak and silver-washed fritillary. Regular recordings of moths have recognised an impressive 570 species, of which four are nationally scarce. Surveys of other invertebrate groups have similarly registered high numbers.

... continued overleaf ▶

Little owl

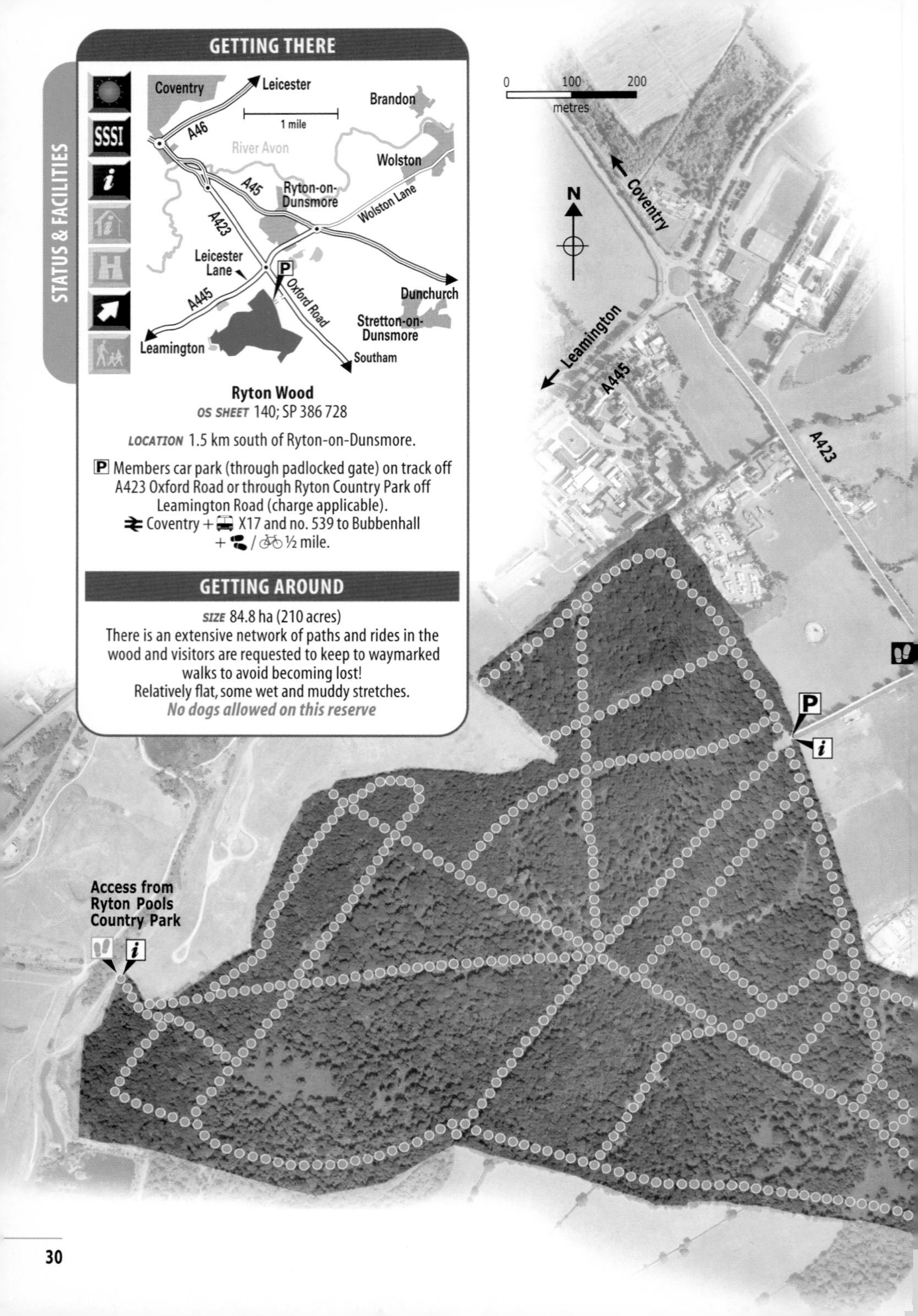
STATUS & FACILITIES
SSSI
GETTING THERE
Coventry
Leicester
Brandon
1 mile
A46
River Avon
Wolston
A45
Ryton-on-
Dunsmore
Wolston Lane
A423
Leicester
Lane
P
Oxford Road
A445
Dunchurch
Stretton-on-
Dunsmore
Leamington
Southam
Ryton Wood
OS SHEET 140; SP 386 728
LOCATION 1.5 km south of Ryton-on-Dunsmore.
P Members car park (through padlocked gate) on track off
A423 Oxford Road or through Ryton Country Park off
Leamington Road (charge applicable).
Coventry + X17 and no. 539 to Bubbenhall
+ / ½ mile.
GETTING AROUND
SIZE 84.8 ha (210 acres)
There is an extensive network of paths and rides in the
wood and visitors are requested to keep to waymarked
walks to avoid becoming lost!
Relatively flat, some wet and muddy stretches.
No dogs allowed on this reserve
0
100
200
metres
N
Coventry
Leamington
A445
A423
P
i
Access from
Ryton Pools
Country Park
i

Cuckoo fledgling

The woodland ponds offer concentrations of both dragonflies and damselflies. Smooth newt, common frog and toad breed here, all providing veritable banquets for the grass snakes regularly seen at the site.

In autumn, fungi and lichens are plentiful, with forays producing long lists with occasional specials, including collared earthstar and silky piggyback. Buzzard and little owl love these exquisite woods and ears and eyes will be well diverted by cuckoo, woodpecker and numerous song birds.

Deer, rabbit and grey squirrel are regularly seen, with red fox, badger, stoat and weasel making for very special, but possible viewing!

MANAGEMENT

Woodland
Traditional management of rotational coppicing with standards; extraction of coppice products for hedgelaying and timber for wood fuel.

Rides
Network of rides and woodland glades are cut on rotation in late summer/early autumn; ride edges are scalloped and the scrub is coppiced on rotation.

Ponds
Encroaching scrub is cut back to prevent it shading the water and invading reed is removed to stop the ponds from drying out.

Waymarked trail
Regularly maintained.

Adder's-tongue

Shadowbrook Meadows

Nestling immediately south of Birmingham International Airport, these beautiful meadows are an age-old part of our cultural heritage – their richness and scarcity recognised with SSSI status. The site falls within the larger designated area of Bickenhill Meadows

Best time to visit

SPRING ✔

PLANTS Cowslip, adder's-tongue, pignut, bird's-foot-trefoil (BELOW)

SUMMER ✔

PLANTS Quaking-grass, crested dog's-tail, betony, meadowsweet, meadow thistle, oxeye daisy
INSECTS Common blue and small copper butterflies, chimney sweeper moth (BELOW)

AUTUMN ✔

FUNGI Meadow waxcap (BELOW) and other waxcaps

WINTER

A small stream bisects the reserve and sumptuous hedgerows divide the site further into two dry meadows, occupying the eastern side of the reserve, and two wet meadows which lie to the west.

Unfertilised, unsprayed and unploughed, the meadows' diversity has been maintained over centuries by the unaltered, traditional hay-cutting and grazing regime.

Especially colourful in June and July, both wet and dry meadows give rise to swathes of wild flowers typical of their habitats. Delights such as meadowsweet, betony and the very local meadow thistle can be discovered in the damper meadows, which flood regularly in the winter. Cowslip, oxeye daisy and pignut create a medley of colour in the company of heath spotted-orchids and a delightful mix of grasses including quaking-grass and crested dog's-tail, which love the drier eastern meadows.

On bright summer days, visits are rewarded with an abundance of butterflies, mating, egg-laying and drinking nectar amongst the flowers. Common blue and small copper butterflies join meadow specialities such as chimney-sweeper moth and six other nationally scarce insects.

In autumn, several species of waxcap fungi fruit well at the reserve, along with many mushrooms. The mature hedgerows, estimated to be approximately 600 years old, add considerably to the diversity of Shadowbrook Meadows. The tall trees are surrounded by shorter vegetation, which forms ideal habitat for a host of small mammals and birds by providing many feeding, hunting and nesting opportunities.

MANAGEMENT

A hay cut is taken in late summer each year with the cut sward removed.

GETTING THERE

STATUS & FACILITIES

SSSI

Shadowbrook Meadow
OS SHEET 139; SP 187 814

LOCATION 1.5 km west of Hampton in Arden. Turn off the B4438 onto Shadowbrook Lane. Access on north side of Shadowbrook Lane.

P Limited parking on Shadowbrook Lane.
Hampton-in-Arden + bus No. 192 to Catherine-de-Barnes + walk / cycle 1¼ miles or 1½ miles from station.

GETTING AROUND

SIZE 4.4 ha (10.9 acres)
Relatively flat, soft patches, access over stile.
Please keep to field boundaries.
No dogs allowed on this reserve

N

Common frog

Swift Valley

Occupying a site on the outskirts of Rugby, close to residential housing and industrial estates, this charming reserve feels surprisingly tucked away in old countryside

Best time to visit

WINTER ✔

BIRDS Ducks, mute swan (BELOW), snipe, gulls

SPRING ✔

INSECTS Holly blue butterfly
AMPHIBIANS Smooth newt, common frog, toad (BELOW)
BIRDS Kestrel, buzzard, coot, moorhen, lapwing
MAMMALS Badger, fox

SUMMER ✔

PLANTS Yellow water-lily, celery-leaved buttercup, meadowsweet, water figwort, gipsywort, skullcap, branched bur-reed, meadow crane's-bill, musk mallow
INSECTS Butterflies, small red-eyed damselfly, southern hawker (BELOW) and other dragonflies
BIRDS Hobby, sparrowhawk

AUTUMN

The reserve's traditional pasture, small woods, hedges and landscaped wetlands offer substantial diversity. The adjoining River Swift, two pools, marshy floodplain and the bordering disused arm of the Oxford Canal add further interest.

Almost completely covered in ancient ridge and furrow plough markings, the land has since been left unploughed and has a long history as grazing pasture. Its calcareous clay soils, with sandy deposits, support species-poor, coarse grassland with red fescue and Yorkshire-fog making up the principle grasses. More pleasing flowers grow here, such as meadow crane's-bill, musk mallow and goat's-beard.

Oak is most abundant in the recently extended woodland, where snowdrop and daffodil have been introduced, offering pretty springtime displays. Wetter areas support woodland of alder and willow. Ash and willow add height to the predominantly hawthorn hedgerows, with occasional turkey oak along the redundant canal.

The marsh is rich and colourful, though not easily explored, and supports many plants including meadowsweet, wild angelica and a mass of rushes and sedges. Smaller plants like gipsywort, water figwort and skullcap also relish these damp conditions.

The wetland habitats of the reserve are ideal for many dragonfly and damselfly species, with small red-eyed damselfly choosing Swift Valley – its first county site – in 2004. Nationally scarce soldier and longhorn beetles have even been recorded. Butterflies are also plentiful in the grassland, especially browns and skippers. Small copper and holly blue appear, while small tortoiseshell, peacock and red admiral benefit from all the nettles. The chimney-sweeper moth breeds here, laying its eggs on the pignut where fat caterpillars later emerge.

Pool margins give rise to bulrush and branched bur-reed, and a scramble of common duckweed forms a blanket on the open water.

... continued overleaf ▶

Yellow water-lily

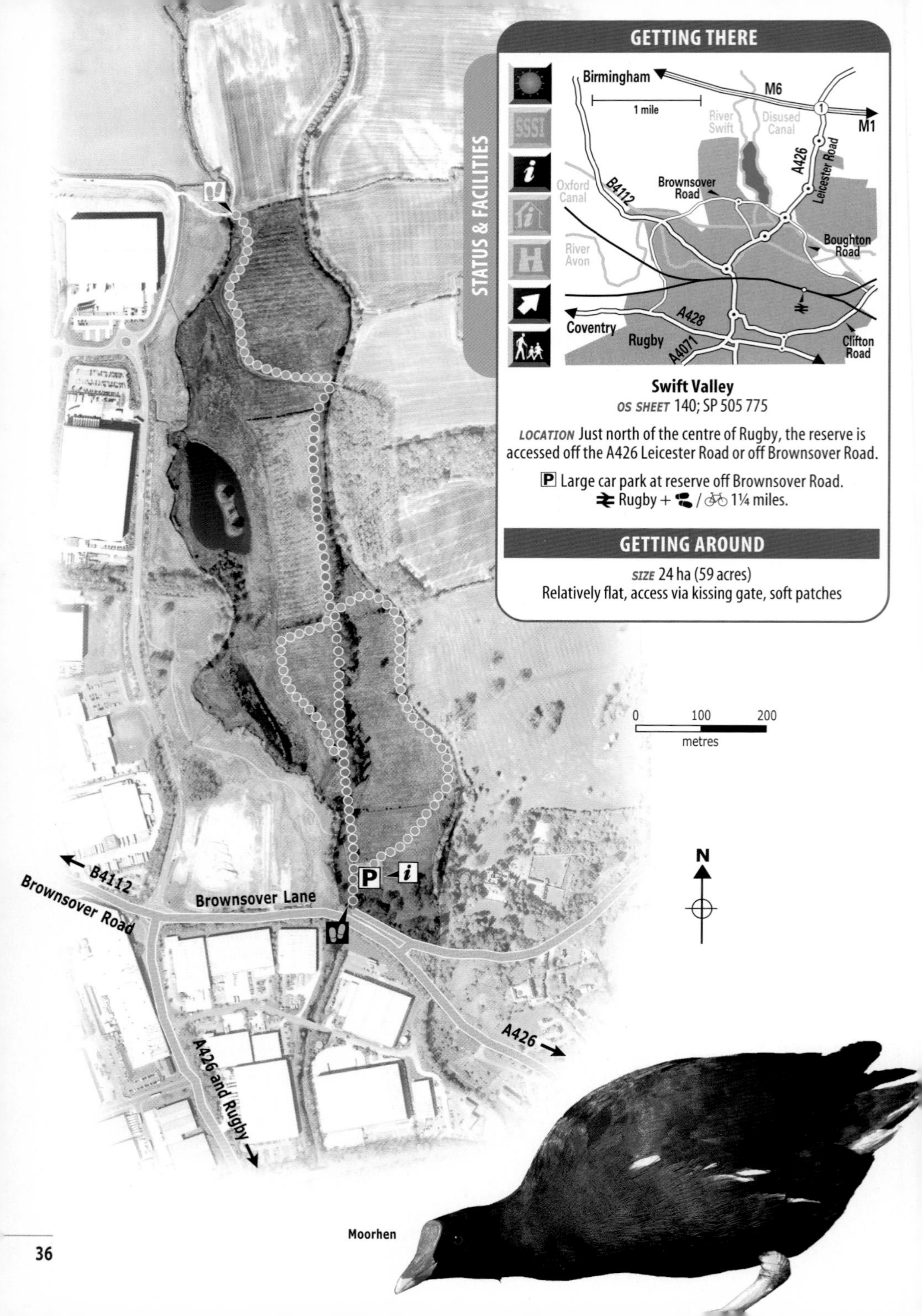

GETTING THERE

Swift Valley

OS SHEET 140; SP 505 775

LOCATION Just north of the centre of Rugby, the reserve is accessed off the A426 Leicester Road or off Brownsover Road.

P Large car park at reserve off Brownsover Road.
Rugby + / 1¼ miles.

GETTING AROUND

SIZE 24 ha (59 acres)
Relatively flat, access via kissing gate, soft patches

Moorhen

Highland cattle

Celery-leaved buttercup

The canal, lovely in summer, expands the list of plants further with yellow water-lily, watercress and celery-leaved buttercup relishing the muddy edges, trampled by grazing highland cattle.

Home to an excellent diversity of birds, the reserve boasts kestrel, hobby and sparrowhawk, which can regularly be seen hunting. Mute swans breed on the wetland as do mallard, tufted duck, coot, moorhen, lapwing and reed bunting. Snipe and various gulls visit the site in winter.

Rabbits and grey squirrel are numerous, with indications of red fox and mole. The rough grasslands hide a multitude of mice, voles and shrews, whose high pitched squeaking can often be heard.

MANAGEMENT

Grassland
Cattle grazed for most of the year with livestock moved between fields; undesirable species such as creeping thistle are controlled.

Marsh
Lightly grazed by cattle and scrub removed to prevent further encroachment.

Boundaries
Fences are kept stock-proof and hedgerows managed on rotation by trimming or hedge-laying.

Paths and kissing gates
Regularly maintained.

Woodland
Newly planted areas are monitored.

Man orchid

Ufton Fields

Ufton Fields has a glorious diversity of grassland, scrub, woodland and wetland with large and small pools, truly meriting its SSSI and LNR status

Best time to visit

WINTER ✔

BIRDS Redwing, fieldfare, goldcrest, siskin, bullfinch (BELOW)

SPRING ✔

PLANTS Man and bee orchids, twayblade, lesser celandine, cowslip
AMPHIBIANS Great crested (BELOW) and smooth newts
REPTILES Grass snake
BIRDS Migrant warblers, turtle dove, little grebe, teal, green woodpecker

SUMMER ✔

PLANTS Greater butterfly-orchid, common spotted-orchid, wild basil, yellow bird's-nest (BELOW)
INSECTS Marbled white butterfly, damselflies and dragonflies
BIRDS Buzzard, kestrel, sparrowhawk, spotted flycatcher

AUTUMN ✔

FUNGI False saffron milkcap (BELOW), grey knight, scarlet bonnet, earpick fungus
PLANTS Autumn gentian

Quarried for limestone in the 1950s, waves of low spoil heaps were dumped forming a series of ridges, with pools developing in the troughs between them and larger pools in the voids created by the quarrying. The post-industrial devastation was hidden behind fast-growing, non-native trees, whilst most of the site was left to recolonise naturally.

To this day, the woodland still contains hybrid poplar, grey alder and conifers, with only small numbers of native tree species such as oak and elm. Ground flowers such as lesser celandine are plentiful, as is ground ivy. Yellow bird's-nest can be found under towering Scot's pine and justification for retaining the conifers comes strongly from their associated fungi – scarlet bonnet and earpick fungus with pine, and false saffron milkcap and grey knight under the spruce.

The calcareous, species-rich grassland blends colourful displays of flowers, including cowslip and wild basil amongst many others. The celebrated man orchid makes an appearance with its splendid flower spikes in late May, gracing Ufton Fields with its only presence in Warwickshire and its most north westerly location in Britain. Twayblade, bee orchid, common spotted-orchid and greater butterfly-orchid can all be found.

The wetland supports an excellent list of flora and also supports epiphytic lichens. The margins of the larger, permanent pools allow common reed, bulrush and greater pond-sedge to colonise and although many of the smaller ponds dry out during summer months, they too provide varying aquatic habitats.

Invertebrates prosper at Ufton Fields and were indeed the main reason for its SSSI designation, with 41 species that are nationally scarce. Twenty-eight butterfly species, including marbled white, thrive and 14 species of dragonfly and damselfly add further spectacles.

... continued overleaf ▶

Broad-bodied chaser

Water life is abundant, with caddisfly larvae, leeches and water-scorpions all to be found lurking in the pools. Common toads breed year on year, producing thousands of toadlets in late spring. Smooth and great crested newts exist in many of the pools, and grass snake is also present.

The bird life is very diverse, with flocks of tits and finches relishing the reserve, along with migrant warblers and spotted flycatcher. Dense scrub provides cover for turtle dove and winter thrushes. Alder attracts siskin, and goldcrests can be viewed amongst the conifers.

Little grebe and teal occupy the pools, with perhaps a passage common sandpiper feeding at the pool margins. Buzzard, kestrel and sparrowhawk hunt the reserve, whilst green woodpeckers search the grassland for ants.

Rabbit, grey squirrel, muntjac and red fox all make a living here, with small rodents and shrews extremely abundant in the longer grass. Several species of bat can be easily viewed on summer evenings as they feed over the grassland and dark waters of the pools.

MANAGEMENT

Pools
Removal and coppicing of scrub around edges of pools to prevent excessive shading of the water and improve structural diversity.

Grassland
Sward is cut in late summer and the cuttings removed; some tall grass is maintained as good habitat for butterflies and other invertebrates; undesirable species such as creeping thistle and ragwort are controlled.

Scrub
Managed by either removal to prevent further encroachment into the grassland areas or coppicing on rotation to maintain good structural diversity.

Paths
Edges cut regularly to ensure they are accessible.

Warwickshire County Council

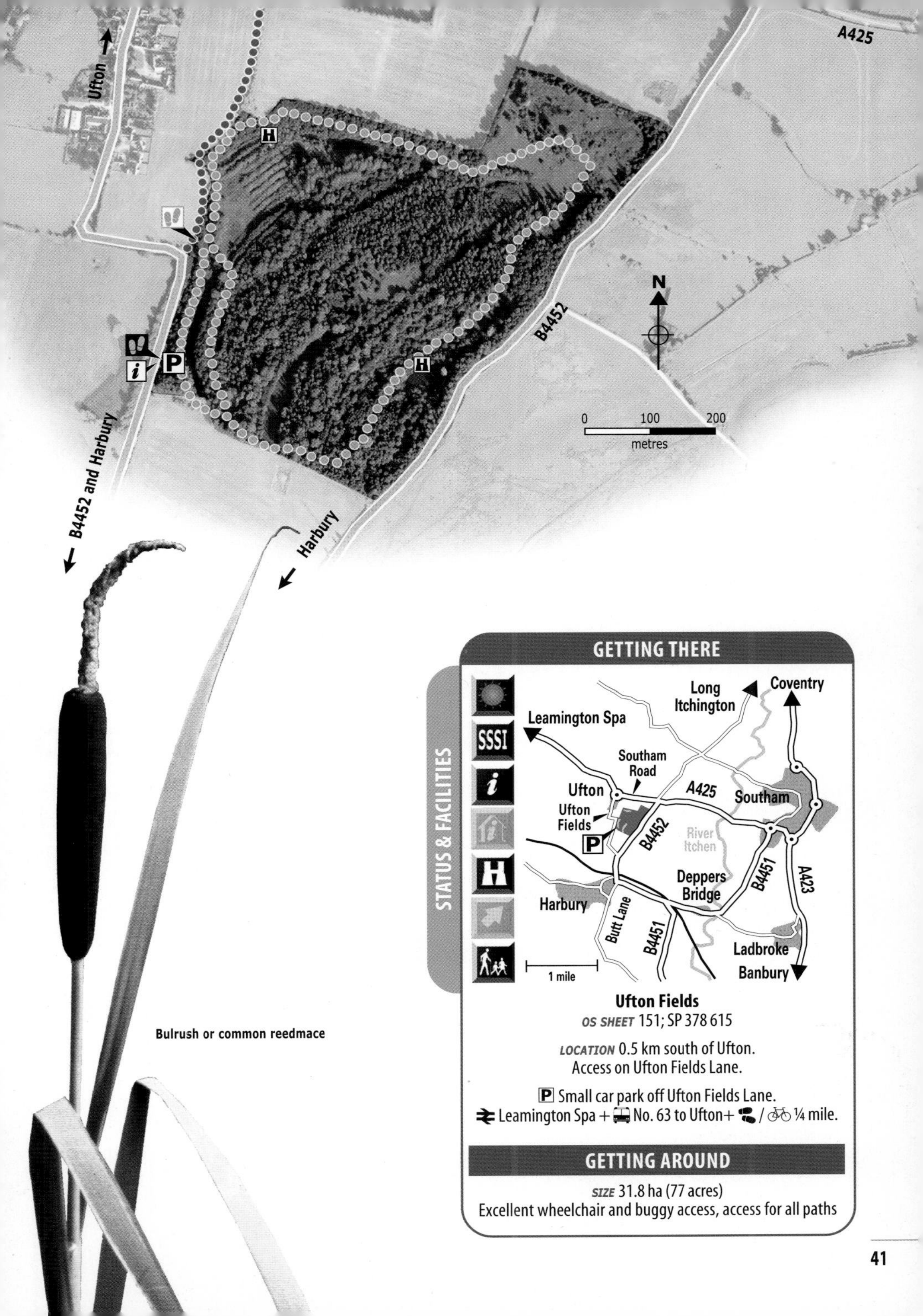

Bulrush or common reedmace

GETTING THERE

Ufton Fields

OS SHEET 151; SP 378 615

LOCATION 0.5 km south of Ufton. Access on Ufton Fields Lane.

P Small car park off Ufton Fields Lane.

Leamington Spa + No. 63 to Ufton + / ¼ mile.

GETTING AROUND

SIZE 31.8 ha (77 acres)

Excellent wheelchair and buggy access, access for all paths

White admiral

Wappenbury Wood and Old Nun Wood

Found at the heart of the Princethorpe woodlands, Wappenbury Wood's ancient history can be traced as far back as 1208, and has probably been forest since the last ice age

Best time to visit

SPRING ✓

PLANTS Bluebell, primrose, wood anemone, wood-sorrel, sanicle, yellow archangel (BELOW), three-veined sandwort, broom, gorse, bitter vetchling, ragged-robin
BIRDS Warblers, woodpeckers, tawny owl

SUMMER ✓

PLANTS Wood sage, marsh thistle, devil's-bit scabious, honeysuckle (BELOW), slender St John's-wort, common spotted-orchid, broad-leaved helleborine
INSECTS White admiral and purple hairstreak butterflies

AUTUMN ✓

FUNGI Oak mazegill, boletes, brittle caps, cinnabar oysterling (BELOW)
PLANTS Leaf and bracken colour

WINTER

Mentioned in the Domesday Book, records show that Richard of Wappenbury was given modest rights over the woods. By the end of the 15th Century, the wood was known by its present name and provided a source of fuel, building materials and hunting opportunities for the local community.

Medieval ridge and furrow plough markings found to the north of the woods, ancient bank boundaries, and the age-old pathway known as Nunwood Lane all provide further evidence of the woods' age. Nearly clear-felled twice in the 1940s and 1950s, the wood was left to regenerate naturally, helping to increase diversity and contributing to its ecological excellence today. Now, with their network of grassy rides and glades, these beautiful woods offer tranquil walks through a wildlife treasure trove.

Lying on heavy soils derived from Triassic mud and sandstone, Wappenbury Wood is made up of oak, ash and hazel with some silver birch and aspen. Crab apple and hawthorn are common, plus field maple, holly and some small-leaved lime in the south-east corner. The damper margins around the brook support willow in the north.

Plant life here is rich and diverse. Spring brings bluebell and primrose, which litter the dappled floor, vying for space with a jumble of wood anemone, wood-sorrel, sanicle, yellow archangel and three-veined sandwort. Broad-leaved helleborine, uncommon in the county, is a notable species. Honeysuckle scrambles through the wood, attracting a multitude of insects and filling the air with its heady aroma on warm summer evenings. Damper, grassy rides are home to common spotted-orchid, marsh thistle, ragged-robin and devil's-bit scabious and are flanked by a tangle of bramble, field rose and dog rose. Gorse and broom flourish in sandy places with wood sage, slender St John's-wort and bitter vetchling. Further delights such as meadow vetchling, yellow rattle, red bartisia and pignut can be found in the remnant meadow.

... continued overleaf ▶

Crab apple blossom

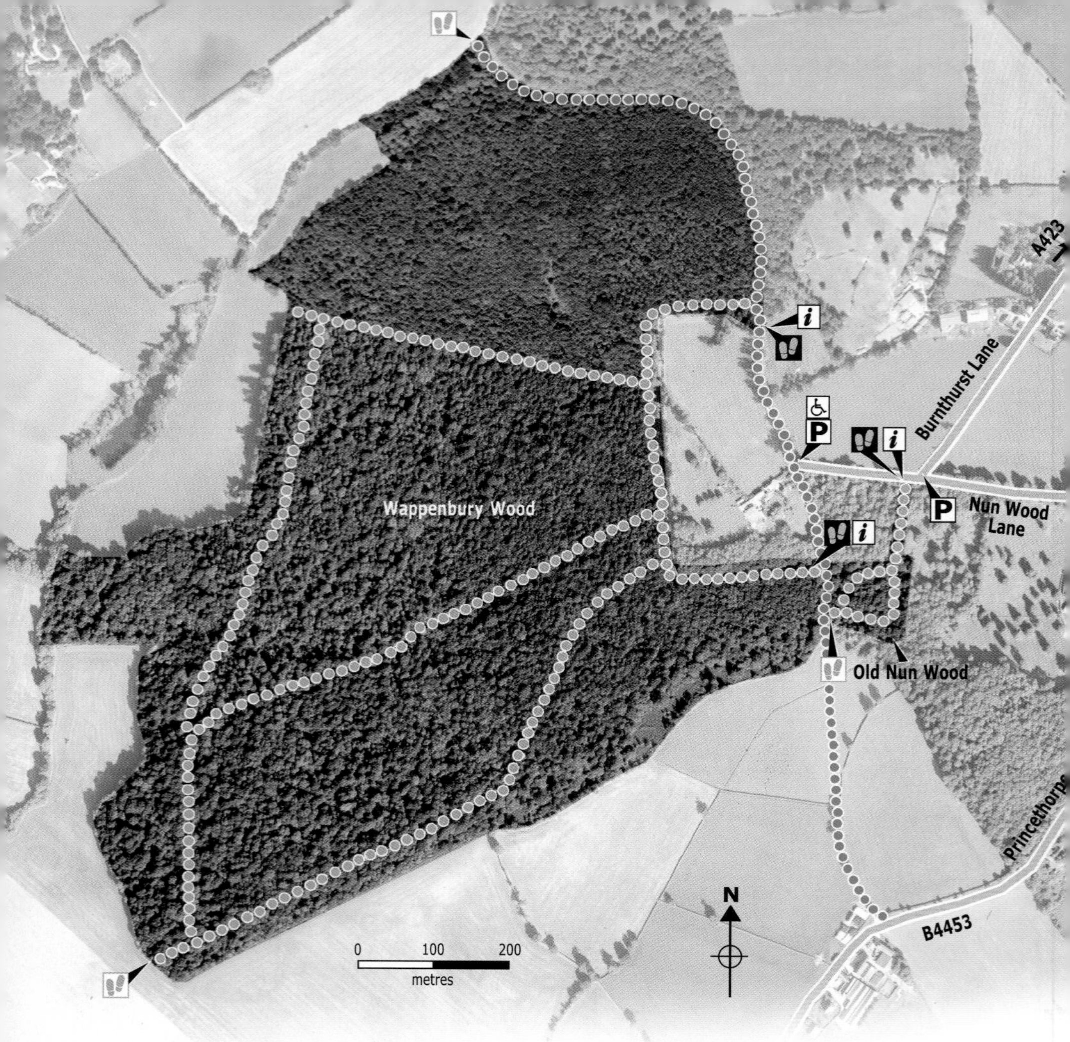

Home to an impressive list of butterflies, the reserve supports white admiral, purple hairstreak and Essex skipper, with a small number of silver-washed fritillary. The narrow-bordered five-spot burnet moth is also found here.

Historically, an impressive 88 species of birds have been recorded, with plentiful sightings of warblers, woodpeckers and tawny owl.

The wood is magical during autumn months with its spectacular display of colour. A technicoloured canopy shields dense bracken and plentiful fungi, including boletes, brittle caps and oak mazegill. The cinnabar oysterling fungus has even been recorded here – its second known location in Britain. Ferns, mosses and liverworts are also well represented.

Old Nun Wood adjoins Wappenbury Wood and connects to Princethorpe Great Wood. It has similar longevity and ecology to that of Wappenbury, although it is much smaller and less diverse. With its winter stream, this little wood adds sweet chestnut and a rare fungus or two to Wappenbury's impressive list.

GETTING THERE

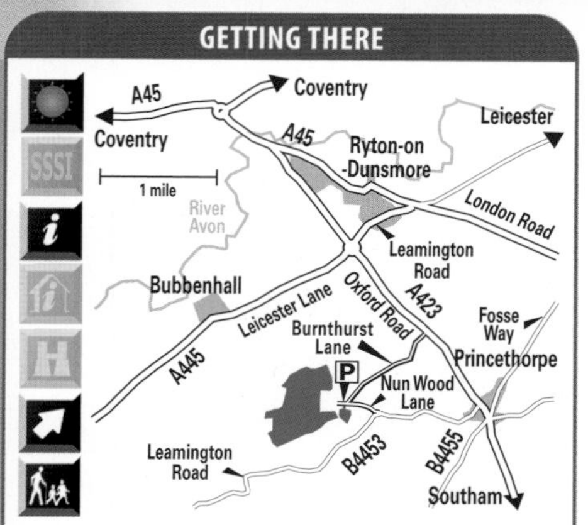

Wappenbury Wood and Old Nun Wood
OS SHEET 140; SP 381 709 & SP 382 708

LOCATION 2 km west of Princethorpe, to the north-east of Leamington Spa. Turn off the A423 onto Burnthurst Lane. The woodland is closed on Wednesdays and Saturdays. The Public Bridleway that partly cuts through the wood is open at all times.

P Park at the junction with Burnthurst and Nun Wood Lane.
Coventry + No. 538
+ / 1½ miles.

GETTING AROUND

SIZE 75.6 ha (186 acres)
Excellent wheelchair and buggy access, access for all paths, some paths along rides get very wet and muddy
No dogs allowed on this reserve except along bridleway where they must be kept on short leads at all times

Woodland mammals are numerous in both woods and sightings of rabbit, grey squirrel and muntjac deer can well be expected. Mole, fox, badger and several other mammals are visitors to these fantastic woods, but only afford rare sightings.

MANAGEMENT

Woodland
Traditional management of rotational coppicing with standards; extraction of coppice products for hedgelaying and timber for wood fuel. Charcoal burning also takes place.

Rides
Network of rides and woodland glades are cut in late summer/early autumn; ride edges are cut back and the scrub is coppiced on rotation.

Paths and waymarked trail
Regularly maintained.

Purple hairstreak

Little grebe

Whitacre Heath

Situated in the Tame Valley, lying on the floodplain of the adjoining River Tame, Whitacre Heath is a complex medley of shallow pools, wetland, woodland and grassland

Best time to visit

WINTER ✔

BIRDS Snipe, tufted duck
MAMMALS Stoat (BELOW)

SPRING ✔

PLANTS Red campion
REPTILES Grass snake
BIRDS Migrant warblers, tits, finches, thrushes, kingfisher (BELOW), little grebe, lesser spotted woodpecker

SUMMER ✔

PLANTS Southern marsh-orchid, common spotted-orchid, blue fleabane (BELOW)
INSECTS Butterflies, dragonflies, emerald damselfly

AUTUMN ✔

BIRDS Lapwing (BELOW)

One of a regionally important chain of wetland sites along the river Tame, the reserve makes up an important part of the Trust's large area Tame Valley Project. Used for sand and gravel extraction in the 1960s, parts of the workings were in-filled and the site was restored for agricultural use in later years. Designated an SSSI, the site is of immense value to an abundance of wildlife, particularly birds.

Regardless of the decline in open water at the site in recent years, the wetland of predominantly reed sweet-grass and common reed attracts an outstanding number of birds. Over 140 species have been recorded since the early 1980s, including kingfisher, redshank, skylark and little grebe. Jack snipe are also occasionally seen in winter.

The woodland habitat contains a mixed population of breeding finches, tits and thrushes, whilst lesser spotted woodpeckers are regular visitors.

Ungrazed damp areas support a large area of reed canary-grass with greater pond-sedge and bulrush. The drier parts give rise to more floristic displays of red campion and the uncommon blue fleabane amongst a sea of grasses including Yorkshire-fog and tufted hair-grass.

The woodland, dominated by alder and willow, hides plenty of mosses and liverworts, which thrive in its damp, shaded parts. Guelder-rose makes a showing with pink purslane and common spotted-orchid.

An invertebrate survey in 2000 identified 1,145 species, of which substantial numbers are nationally scarce. Twenty-five species of butterfly have been recorded, including brown argus and white-letter hairstreak. The reserve attracts many delightful dragonflies and damselflies, such as the impressive emperor dragonfly and the small but startling emerald damselfly.

... continued overleaf ▶

Grass snake

Amphibians and reptiles relish the moist habitat and grass snakes seek refuge amongst the reeds.

The dry grasslands are heavily browsed by rabbits, providing regular pickings for fox and stoat. Bats are regular feeders at this beautiful reserve and can be seen feeding near the woodland and over the pools.

MANAGEMENT

Wet grassland
Low intensity cattle grazing in summer through to the autumn.

Wet woodland
Thinning and pollarding of willows to improve structural diversity; removal of non-native Himalyan balsam.

Boundaries
Fences are kept stock-proof.

Paths and hides
Regular cutting back of vegetation to keep pathways open. Hides maintained in a good state of repair

Common spotted-orchid

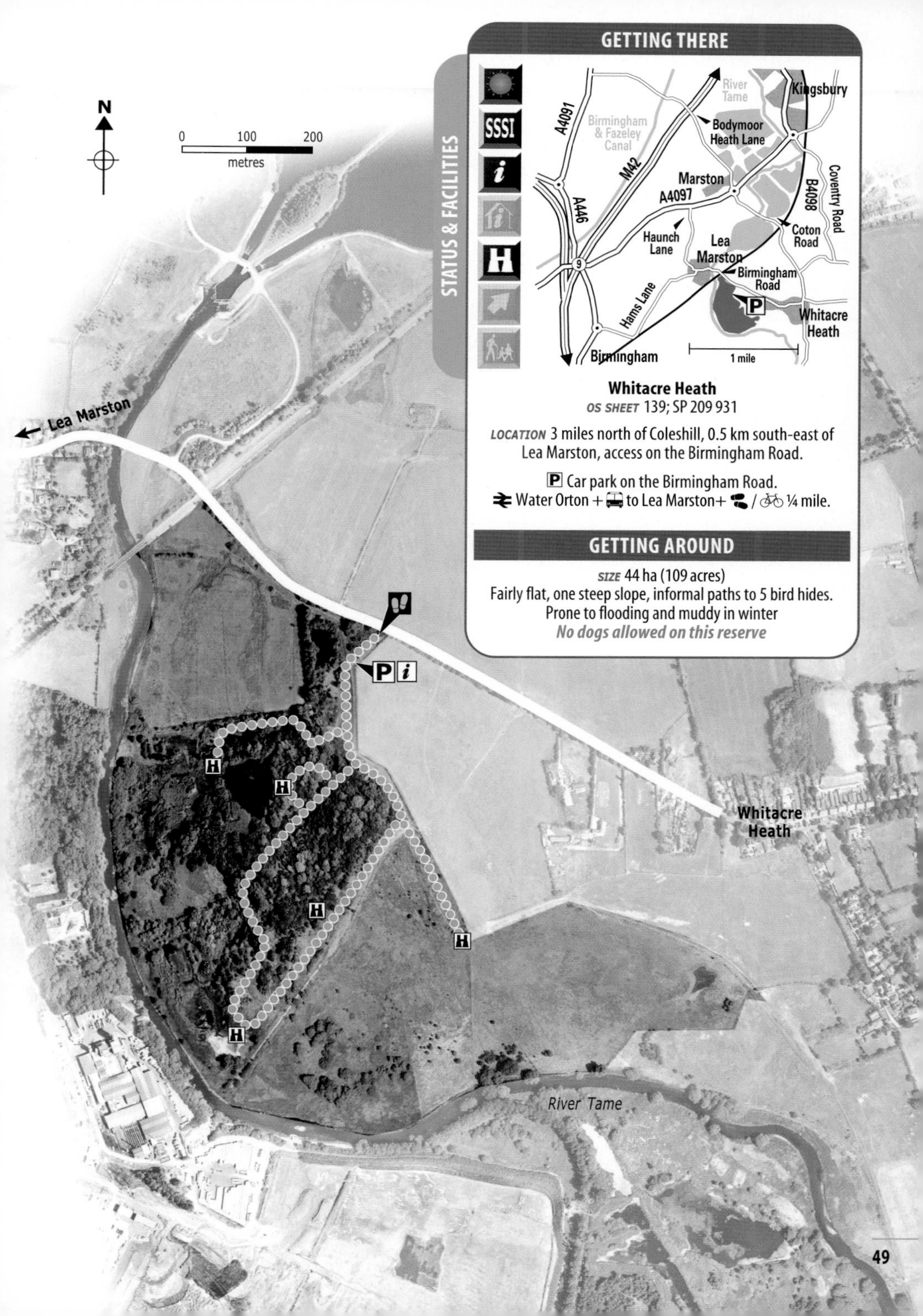

Whitacre Heath

OS SHEET 139; SP 209 931

LOCATION 3 miles north of Coleshill, 0.5 km south-east of Lea Marston, access on the Birmingham Road.

P Car park on the Birmingham Road.
Water Orton + bus to Lea Marston + walk / cycle ¼ mile.

GETTING AROUND

SIZE 44 ha (109 acres)
Fairly flat, one steep slope, informal paths to 5 bird hides.
Prone to flooding and muddy in winter
No dogs allowed on this reserve

Grass vetchling

Ashlawn Cutting

Slicing through lias clay soils, this superb railway cutting holds a splendid collection of flowering plants

Best time to visit

WINTER ✔

PLANTS Gorse (BELOW)
BIRDS Redwing, fieldfare

SPRING ✔

PLANTS Cowslip, violets
AMPHIBIANS Frogs and frog spawn (BELOW)
REPTILES Grass snake
BIRDS Chiffchaff, willow warbler, moorhen

SUMMER ✔

PLANTS Grass vetchling, fairy flax, agrimony, fool's water-cress
INSECTS Brown argus, white-letter hairstreak, comma, peacock and marbled white (BELOW) butterflies, forester moth, dragonflies
BIRDS Reed bunting
MAMMALS Badger signs

AUTUMN

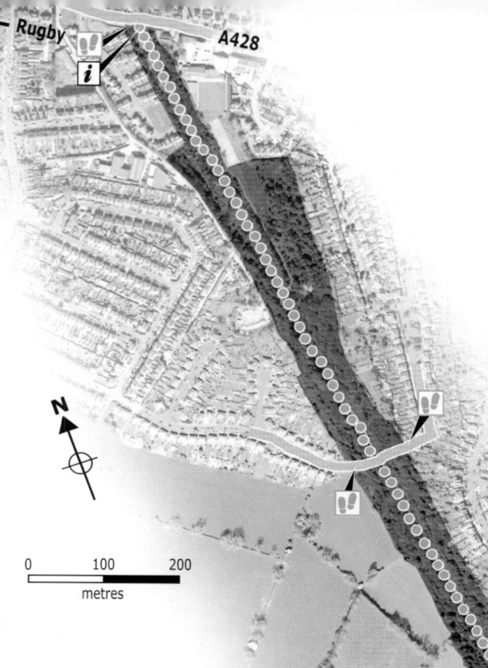

Surrounded by agriculturally improved farmland and housing on the outskirts of Rugby, this reserve, with its steep banks of calcareous grassland, scrub and pools, now forms the only extensive natural area for wildlife in the local countryside.

Areas of unimproved grassland rich with grass vetchling, fairy flax and agrimony provide excellent cover for small mammals and insects, of which nine are nationally notable. Twenty-two butterfly species including marbled white and brown argus are recorded here, with Ashlawn Cutting being the only location for forester moth in Warwickshire.

The invasive hawthorn scrub invites a large population of finches, thrushes, starlings and sparrows, with reed bunting enjoying the damper habitat around the ponds which supports great willowherb, fool's water-cress and the occasional bulrush.

Dragonflies prosper here as do frogs, toads and newts, providing an ideal food source for grass snakes that are occasionally seen.

GETTING THERE

STATUS & FACILITIES

Rugby
A426
B5414
A428
A4071
Coventry
Hillmorton
Hillmorton Road
Barby Road
Ashlawn Road
B4429
Onley Lane
Southam
½ mile
M45

Ashlawn Cutting

OS SHEET 140; SP 516 732

LOCATION ½ mile south from the centre of Rugby. Take the A428 Hillmorton Road, turn onto the B4429 Ashlawn Road and park at the reserve entrance.

P Car park on Ashlawn Road (B4429).
Rugby + / 2 miles.

GETTING AROUND

SIZE 22 ha (54 acres)
Flat, good wheelchair access to bottom of the cutting at Onley Lane. Steep sides elsewhere. Floods in winter

B4429
Southam

MANAGEMENT

Management focuses on cutting back some of the invasive hawthorn scrub on the embankment to maintain the grassland areas for butterflies.

Great burnet

Brook Meadow

This traditional, species-rich hay meadow is surrounded by hedgerows of mature trees and shrubs – Cuttle Brook forms the western boundary, flooding or water-logging the field each winter on its way to Temple Balsall Nature Reserve

Best time to visit

WINTER 

MAMMALS Brown hare (BELOW)

SPRING ✓

PLANTS Marsh-marigold, blackthorn (BELOW) and wild plum blossom, meadow foxtail, sweet vernal-grass

SUMMER ✓

PLANTS Ragged-robin, great burnet, lesser water-parsnip, devil's-bit scabious, brooklime, meadow thistle (BELOW), pendulous sedge
MAMMALS Badger signs

AUTUMN ✓

PLANTS Hedgerow colour, spindle fruit (BELOW)

Formed on alluvial soil, this meadow is designated as an SSSI for its herb-rich flood meadow grassland, characterised by meadow foxtail and great burnet, now very scarce in the county. The wetter northern end of the reserve proffers marsh-marigold and wild angelica, and even the rare meadow thistle enjoys refuge amongst a bevy of companions.

Sixteen species of grass have been identified including crested dog's-tail, sweet vernal-grass and yellow oat-grass, all hiding wild flowers including devil's-bit scabious and meadow vetchling.

The meadow's boundaries comprise oak, ash and field maple with Scots pine towering over hazel, wild plum and blackthorn. This offers suitable cover for many inhabitants, including brown hare during the winter months.

The stream's margin adds alder, willow and white poplar, with brooklime and lesser water-parsnip flourishing in the water alongside an abundance of the tall pendulous sedge.

MANAGEMENT

Management of this meadow involves taking a hay crop in summer, aftermath grazing with cattle and maintaining the reserve boundaries.

GETTING THERE

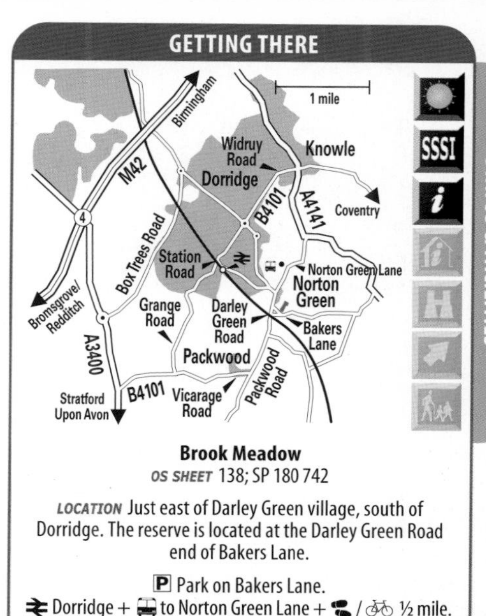

Brook Meadow

OS SHEET 138; SP 180 742

LOCATION Just east of Darley Green village, south of Dorridge. The reserve is located at the Darley Green Road end of Bakers Lane.

P Park on Bakers Lane.

Dorridge + bus to Norton Green Lane + walk / cycle ½ mile.

GETTING AROUND

SIZE 2 ha (5 acres)

Relatively flat, no defined paths, prone to waterlogging, please stick to boundary

No dogs allowed on this reserve

Devil's-bit scabious

Emperor dragonfly

Claybrookes Marsh

This urban nature reserve has developed its conservation value as a result of its past industrial use

Best time to visit

SPRING ✔

AMPHIBIANS Toad, common frog, smooth newt
BIRDS Reed warbler (BELOW), sedge warbler, reed bunting

SUMMER ✔

PLANTS Bird's-foot-trefoil, hare's-foot clover, purple-loosestrife, tutsan, yellow loosestrife, common spotted-orchid (BELOW), southern marsh-orchid
INSECTS Dragonflies, hoverflies

WINTER

AUTUMN

Originally grassland and a natural marsh, Binley colliery railhead was constructed on the site in 1910, closing by 1963.

Later, industrial development was forestalled by discoveries of 49 nationally and regionally scarce insects, and the site was given SSSI status, saving it from destruction.

The reserve offers a splendid range of habitats to a host of wildlife. Bare ground provides a range of weedy plants and sanctuary for bees, wasps and beetles. Grassland, with flowers such as bird's-foot-trefoil and hare's-foot clover and drifts of Yorkshire-fog attract local butterfly species such as marbled white and small heath. Common spotted-orchid, yellow loosestrife and tutsan add further botanical diversity.

Extensive reedbeds allow cover for breeding reed bunting and reed warbler and provide ideal habitat for southern marsh-orchids to flower.

Small pools display a dozen dragonfly species in June and hide common frog, toad and smooth newt amongst the purple-loosestrife, rushes and reeds.

GETTING THERE

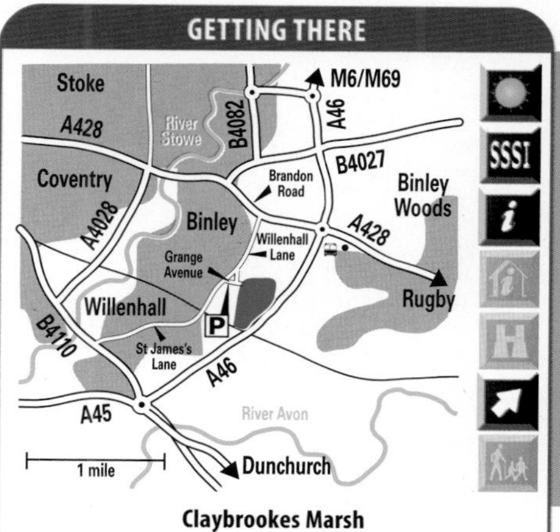

STATUS & FACILITIES

Claybrookes Marsh
OS SHEET 140; SP 380 769

LOCATION On the south-east edge of Coventry. Off the A428 Binley Road, turn south into Willenhall Lane. Turn 3rd left onto Grange Avenue.

P Parking on Grange Avenue and Oak Lane.
Coventry + to Binley Woods + / 1½ miles.

GETTING AROUND

SIZE 10.6 ha (26.2 acres)
Relatively flat, soft patches, floods in winter

MANAGEMENT

Management focuses around clearing the birch regeneration to maintain the grassland areas and cutting the reedbed.

Coventry City Council

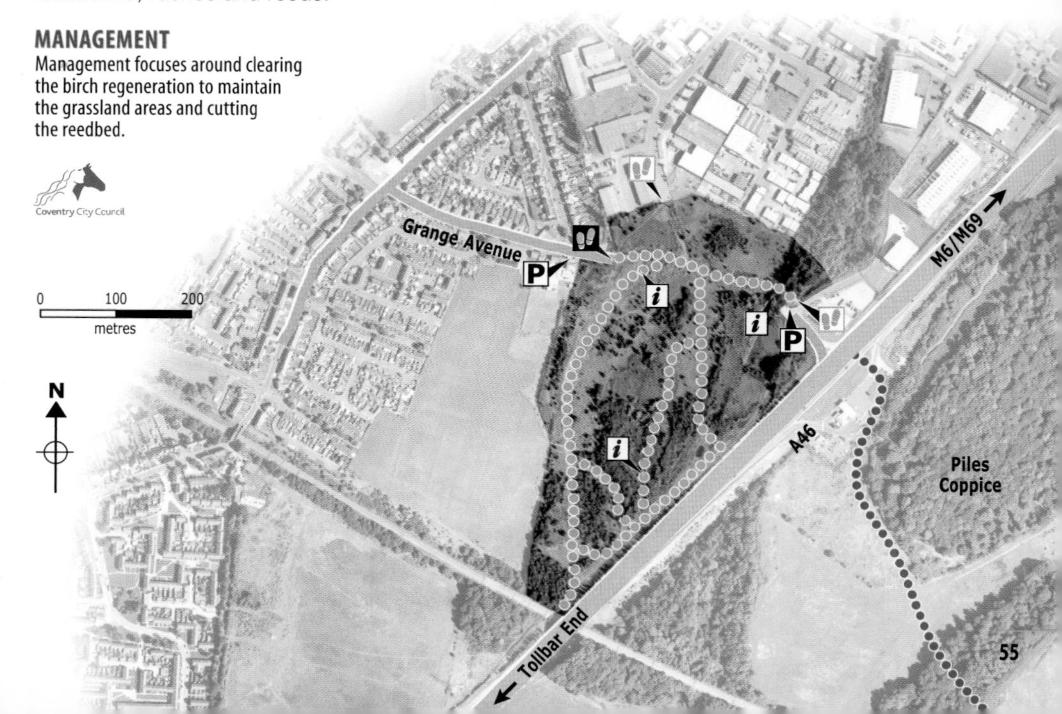

Tawny grisette

Crackley Wood

Once part of the great Forest of Arden, this ancient and attractive wood, known as Crattele in 1154, was included in the Domesday Book as woodland of Stoneleigh Parish

Best time to visit

SPRING ✔

PLANTS Bluebell, wood anemone (BELOW), common dog-violet, opposite-leaved golden-saxifrage, rowan

SUMMER ✔

PLANTS Yellow pimpernel, foxglove, wood sage
INSECTS Hoverflies
BIRDS Tawny owl (BELOW)

AUTUMN ✔

FUNGI Tawny grisette, dog stinkhorn, beefsteak fungus
PLANTS Silver birch, bracken (BELOW), sweet chestnut autumn colour

WINTER

Now a popular LNR, this intriguing woodland offers splendid strolls through an enchanting network of shady paths and grassy, open glades.

Historically coppiced with standards, the practice was abandoned during the last century with the introduction of sweet chestnut, sycamores and conifers. Oaks and silver birch remain the principal species with ash and beech alongside.

May gives rise to a spectacular blanket of bluebells with delicate wood anemone, yellow pimpernel and common dog-violet adding further gems to the woodland floor. Acidic, sandy and clay soils support wood sage, foxglove and bracken, whilst opposite-leaved golden-saxifrage relishes the damper areas.

Under a canopy of vibrant autumn colour an extensive show of fungi provides an impressive spectacle, with tawny grisette, dog stinkhorn and beefsteak fungus abundant.

Rare and nationally uncommon invertebrates such as one species of sawfly and three notable hoverfly species have been recorded here, offering specialists a scarce delight.

MANAGEMENT

The wood is being managed by removal of non-native species, coppicing, and maintenance of rides, ponds, ditches and hedges.

WARWICK DISTRICT COUNCIL

GETTING THERE

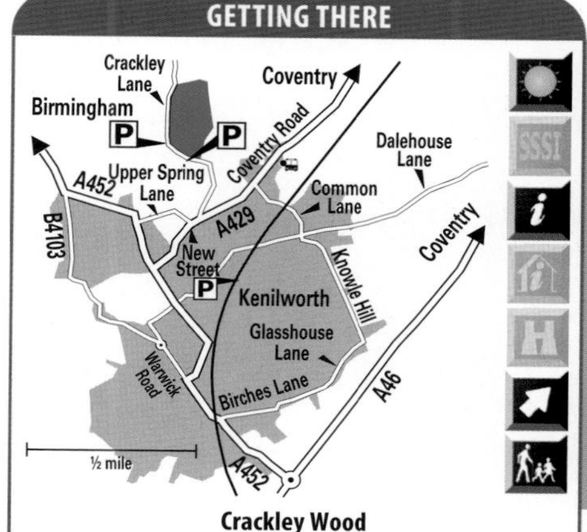

STATUS & FACILITIES

Crackley Wood

OS SHEET 140; SP 290 737

LOCATION Just north of Kenilworth, turn off the A452 onto the A429, take the 2nd left onto Crackley Lane where there are several parking points

P Car parking off Crackley Lane.
Coventry and Leamington Spa stations + bus to Kenilworth + walk / cycle ¾ mile.

GETTING AROUND

SIZE 13.9 ha (34.4 acres)
Flat, circular path

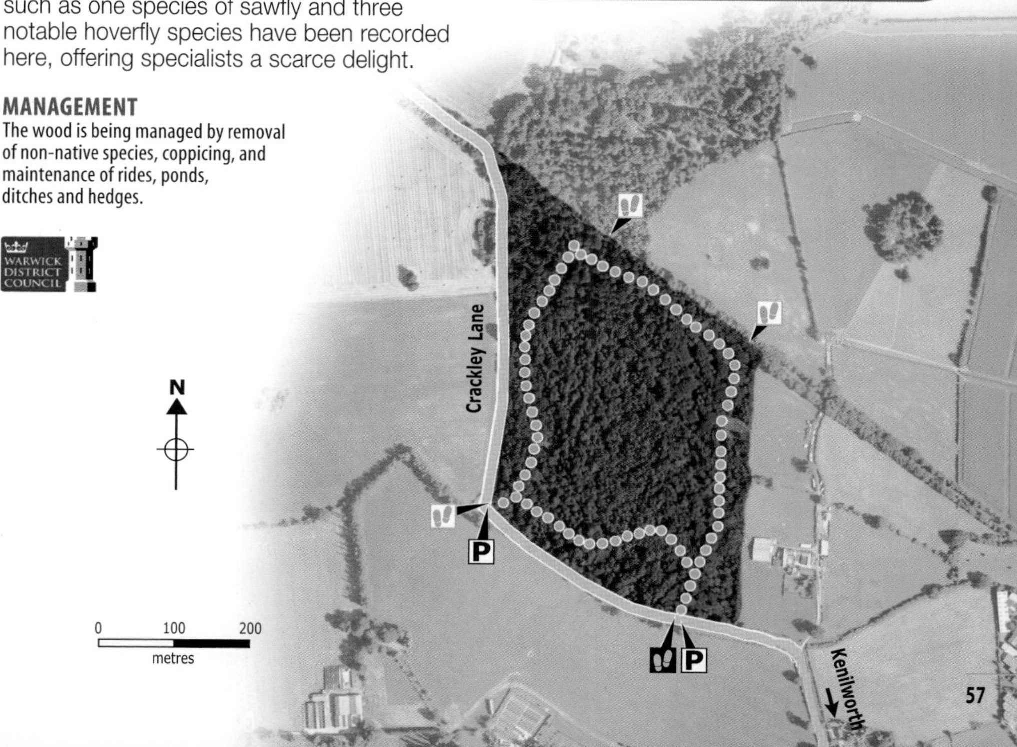

Grizzled skipper butterfly

Grove Hill

One of the largest areas of semi-natural limestone grassland in the county, this rural reserve forms a chequerboard of habitats with large areas of grass, scrub, woodland and ponds

Best time to visit

WINTER ✔

PLANTS Traveller's joy fruits (BELOW)
BIRDS Buzzard, woodpeckers
MAMMALS Muntjac, roe deer

SPRING ✔

PLANTS Cowslip, hairy violet, wild strawberry
INSECTS Brimstone (BELOW) and grizzled skipper butterflies
BIRDS Migrant warblers

SUMMER ✔

PLANTS Common spotted-orchid, bee orchid, pyramidal orchid (BELOW), fairy flax, common gromwell, long-stalked crane's-bill
INSECTS Marbled white and small copper butterflies, burnet moth, white-tailed bumblebee, dragonflies and damselflies

AUTUMN ✔

PLANTS Autumn gentian (BELOW), leaf colour
BIRDS Jay

Lying on a steep scarp slope Grove Hill is abundant with wild privet, dogwood and buckthorn, with dog-rose and traveller's joy scrambling throughout.

Its heavy calcareous Jurassic and Triassic clays give rise to sticky soils, which yield a vast medley of flowers including cowslip, wild strawberry and common gromwell. Smaller plants include hairy violet, fairy flax and long-stalked crane's-bill. Beautiful common spotted-orchid, pyramidal and bee orchids flower here too.

Insects flourish, particularly butterflies including grizzled skipper, brown argus, marbled white, small copper and the striking brimstone. Nationally scarce bees, flies and beetles have been recorded, along with the notable ruddy carpet moth.

One of the two ponds, excavated in 1996, sits towards the north end of the rough grassland and supports emperor and southern hawker dragonflies and the dazzling azure and common blue damselflies.

Birds are equally diverse with woodpeckers, buzzard, sparrowhawk, tawny owl and woodcock. Summer visitors include turtle dove and many species of migrant warbler.

Muntjac and roe deer are often seen foraging here if you tread quietly.

MANAGEMENT

Management is focused on keeping the grassland clear of scrub by manual removal, grazing by sheep and coppicing.

GETTING THERE

Alcester · A46 · Stratford · Croft Lane · Exhall · Wixford · P · Temple Grafton · Ardens Grafton · George's Elm Lane · Grafton Lane · Bidford-on-Avon · B439 · ½ mile

Grove Hill

OS SHEET 150; SP 112 547

LOCATION 2½ miles south-east of Alcester on the road between Exhall and Ardens Grafton. Turn off the A46 Alcester Southern By-pass onto Croft Lane. At crossroads turn right and follow road into Little Britain. The reserve is situated on the right, parking opposite.

P Limited parking available opposite reserve entrance, do not park in gateway.
Stratford-upon-Avon + bus to Grafton Lane + walk / cycle ¼ mile.

GETTING AROUND

SIZE 13.2 ha (33 acres)
Very steep slopes in parts, soft in patches

STATUS & FACILITIES

SSSI

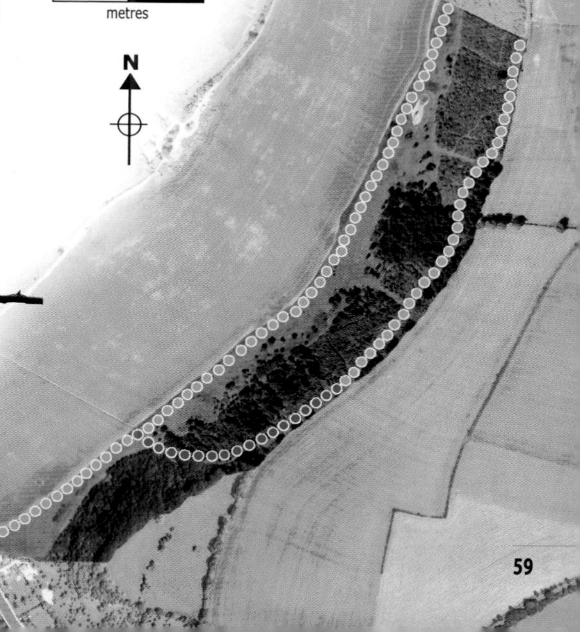

Dog-rose

White-letter hairstreak butterfly

Hampton Wood and Meadow

This splendid ancient wood and flood meadow lying along the River Avon offers outstanding biodiversity with its grassy rides, glades, a shady gully and two streams

Best time to visit

SPRING ✔

FUNGI Morels
PLANTS Primrose, bluebell, wood anemone, lesser celandine, barren strawberry, bugle, yellow archangel
INSECTS Brimstone and comma butterflies
AMPHIBIANS Toad, frog
BIRDS Blackcap (BELOW) and other migrant warblers

SUMMER ✔

PLANTS Hard shield-fern, hart's-tongue, meadowsweet, foxglove
INSECTS Purple hairstreak, white-letter hairstreak, holly blue and white admiral (BELOW) butterflies

AUTUMN ✔

FUNGI Shaggy parasol (BELOW), fly agaric, giant puffball
PLANTS Leaf colour

WINTER ✔

PLANTS Hazel (BELOW)
BIRDS Woodcock, kingfisher, great spotted woodpecker

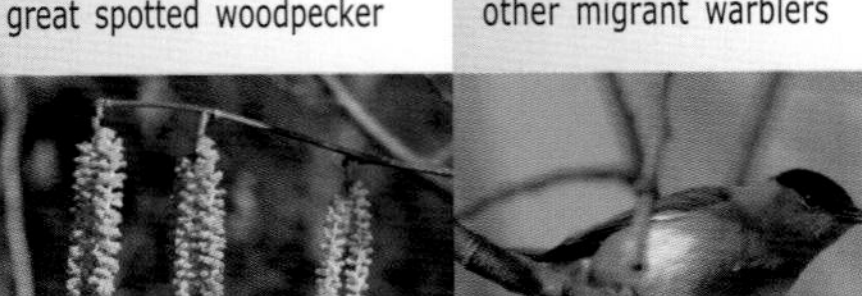

Despite its historical records back to medieval times, Hampton Wood was clear-felled in 1945 and pigs and cattle grazed the area. Following its later neglect, oak woodland re-emerged mixed with many other trees including birch, ash and suckering elm. Hazel re-grew along with blackthorn, crab apple and dogwood.

Boasting a beautiful carpet of wild flowers in spring, the reserve is deservedly famous for its spectacular primroses, which compete with a medley of bluebells, wood anemone and lesser celandine. Red campion and foxglove thrive alongside ground-ivy and yellow archangel, with the grassy rides offering barren strawberry, violets and bugle.

Hard shield-fern and liverworts appear along the stream's banks with hart's-tongue in the gully, and rare lichens grow on some trees. Over 200 species of fungi emerge here, from morels to giant puffball and shaggy parasol.

Twenty-eight butterfly species relish these woods including white-letter and purple hairstreaks, white admiral and holly blue. Over 500 species of beetle have been recorded and the woods are abundant with dragonflies and damselflies.

Birds are numerous with over 30 species recorded during the early summer months. Spring welcomes many warblers and woodcock overwinters here. Kingfishers are regularly seen at this site as they dart into the Avon for fish.

The flood meadow has many wetland and marsh plants including hemlock, creeping buttercup and meadowsweet, and plays home to a colony of breeding toads.

MANAGEMENT

Hampton Wood is managed by cutting to maintain the rides and glades and by coppicing.

SSSI

GETTING THERE

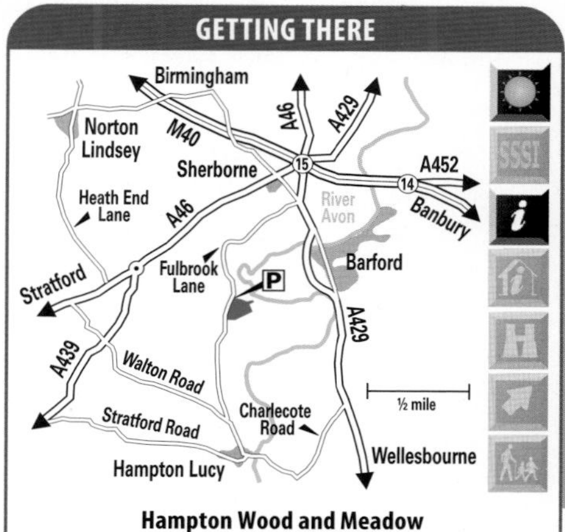

Hampton Wood and Meadow
OS SHEET 151; SP 254 600

LOCATION Situated about half way along Fulbrook Lane between Sherbourne and Hampton Lucy.

P Car park at reserve – **do not park on the road.**
Warwick Parkway and Stratford-upon-Avon + to Hampton Lucy + / 2 miles.

GETTING AROUND

SIZE 12.3 ha (30.3 acres)
Well defined informal paths. The flood meadow becomes wet during winter months and paths within the woodland can become muddy

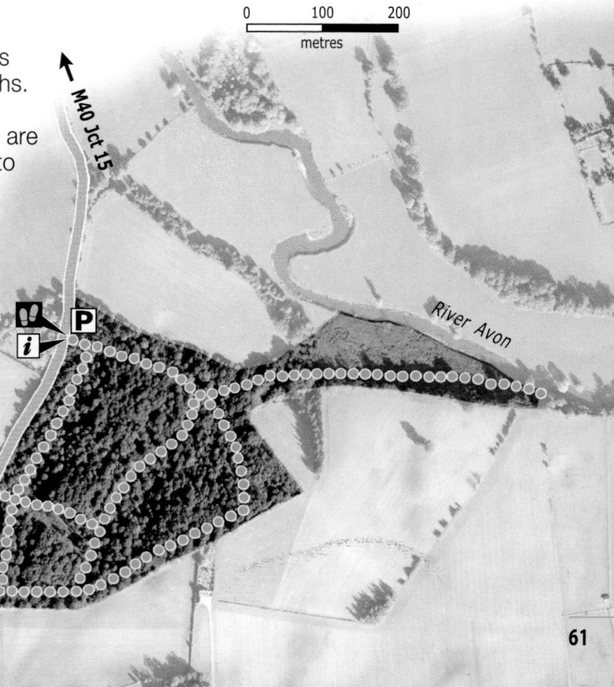

Autumn gentian

Harbury Spoilbank

The spoils from this railway cutting deliver a peaceful mosaic of limestone grassland, superb for flowers and butterflies and is well worthy of its SSSI status

Best time to visit

SPRING ✔

FUNGI Morels
PLANTS Wild strawberry, midland hawthorn, hairy violet, cowslip, early forgetmenot
INSECTS Grizzled skipper, dingy skipper, green hairstreak (BELOW), holly blue, brimstone and orange-tip butterflies
BIRDS Migrant warblers

SUMMER ✔

PLANTS Yellow-wort, dog-rose (BELOW), carline, dwarf and woolly thistles, common spotted-orchid, twayblade
INSECTS Gatekeeper, meadow brown and marbled white butterflies
BIRDS Green woodpecker

WINTER ✔

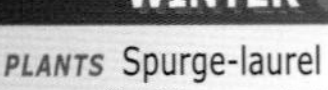

PLANTS Spurge-laurel
BIRDS Fieldfare, redwing (BELOW)

AUTUMN ✔

FUNGI Collared earthstar, cobalt crust
PLANTS Autumn gentian, wild privet fruit (BELOW)

Created from the construction of the Leamington to Oxford railway in the 1840s, the lias clay spoilbanks now host a species-rich grassland dotted with cowslip, early forgetmenot and hairy violet, with wild strawberry, yellow-wort and hoary plantain accompanying. Orchids here include twayblade and common spotted-orchid.

The reserve is notable for over 20 species of butterfly, including an excellent offer of early species such as brimstone, green hairstreak, holly blue and the special grizzled and dingy skippers. A number of scarce county insects have been recorded here at the northerly limit of their British distribution.

In the shade of the dense hawthorn and spurge-laurel, a blanket of dog-violet and moss covers the ground. Scrub graduates into predominantly ash and sycamore woodland, with occasional wild cherry and crab apple all offering residence to a number of spring migrant birds and winter thrushes. Green woodpeckers are common here, often seen feeding from the yellow meadow ant hills found amongst the grass.

Fungi also appear with vernal morels, autumn collared earthstar and the startling cobalt crust making for spectacular viewing.

MANAGEMENT

Maintenance of the calcareous grassland relies on the removal of invading scrub.

GETTING THERE

Harbury Spoilbank

OS SHEET 151; SP 384 598

LOCATION South-west of Southam, turn off the A425 Southam Road onto B4452. Head towards Deppers Bridge, the reserve is on the left.

P Parking limited – on verge next to the Great Western pub.

Leamington Spa + No. 64 to Bishops Itchington + / ¼ mile.

GETTING AROUND

SIZE 6.7 ha (16.6 acres)

Steep slopes with steps, areas prone to waterlogging

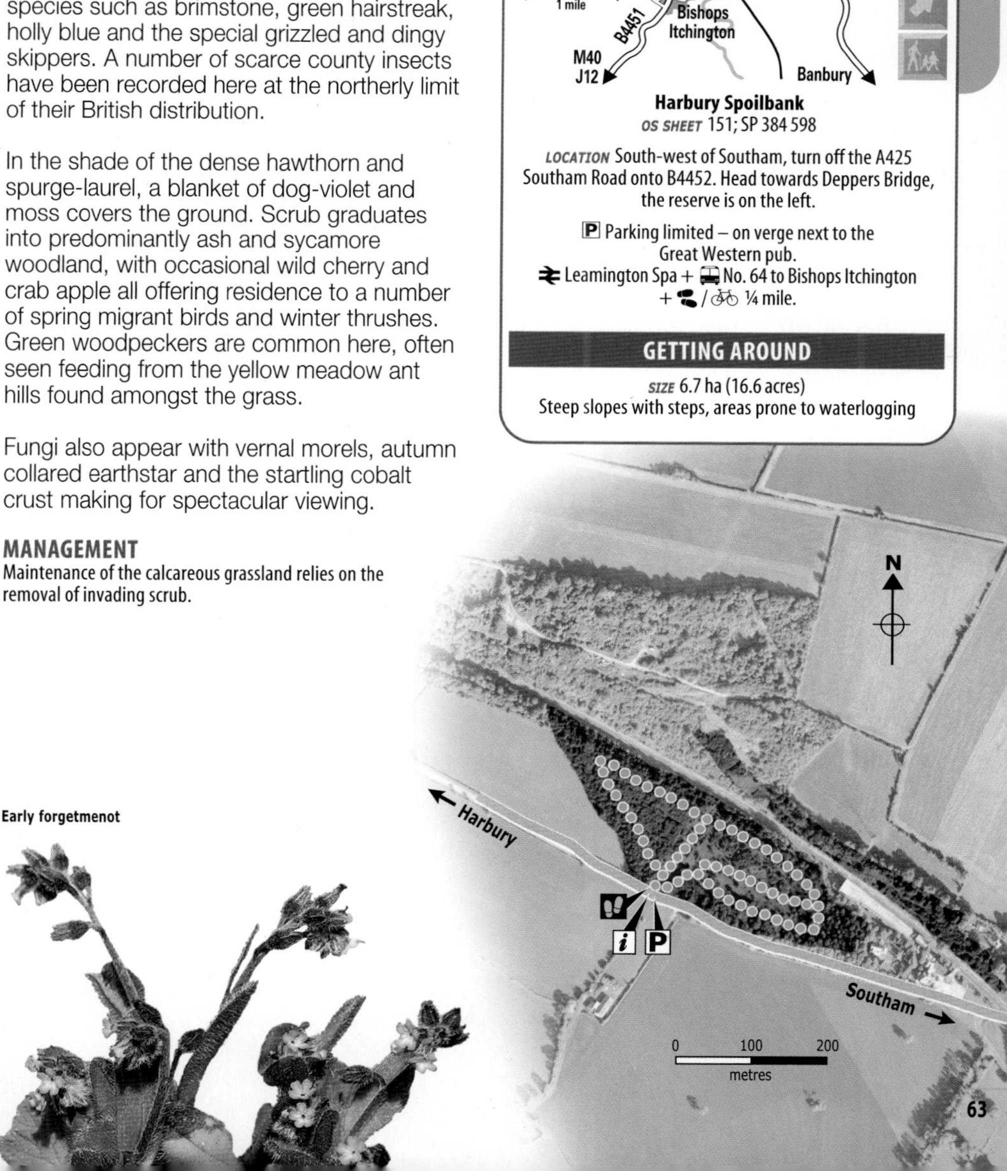

Early forgetmenot

Great spotted woodpecker

Kenilworth Common

This delightfully diverse woodland reserve is enveloped by the historical town of Kenilworth, revealing many secrets of its medieval past

Best time to visit

WINTER ✔
BIRDS Finches, siskin (BELOW), tits, jay, sparrowhawk

SPRING ✔
PLANTS Gorse, broom (BELOW), woodland flowers
REPTILES Slow-worm
BIRDS Kingfisher, woodpeckers

SUMMER ✔
PLANTS Heath bedstraw, wavy hair-grass, common bird's-foot-trefoil
INSECTS Glow-worm (BELOW)
REPTILES Grass snake

AUTUMN ✔
FUNGI Amethyst deceiver, fly agaric (BELOW)
PLANTS Beech leaf and bracken colour

Now a splendid LNR, the Common was created in 1756, providing rough grazing land dominated by typical heathland species and acidic grassland. Following the removal of grazing cattle in the 1800s, the site was colonised by oak and birch, now offering pleasant woodland walks.

Finham Brook babbles along the edge of the reserve, forming its southern boundary. Supporting a diverse range of aquatic invertebrates, the brook provides a rich fishing ground for the spectacular kingfisher, and a natural population of brown trout lurk in its shady waters.

Bisected by the Coventry to Leamington Spa railway, the reserve still retains some remnant heathland, now a rare habitat in Warwickshire. Bracken and wavy hair-grass prosper in areas with broom and heath bedstraw all further reminders of a habitat once common in the county.

Gorse and heather grow outside the reserve on undisturbed slopes where slow-worm and common lizard have been observed.

This reserve brings a delight with every season. Spring flowers punctuate the woodland floor with bursts of colour. Summer welcomes fairytale glow-worms, autumn a range of fungi including amethyst deceiver, ugly milkcap and fly agaric, whilst a crisp winter visit provides clear viewing of colourful finches, tits and jays.

MANAGEMENT

Management of the reserve includes rotational coppicing, removal of invasive species and the maintenance of paths and trails.

GETTING THERE

Birmingham
Coventry
Crackley Lane
A452
Upper Spring Lane
B4103
A429
Woodmill Meadow
Common Lane
Dalehouse Lane
Highland Road
Knowle Hill
Kenilworth
Glasshouse Lane
Warwick Road
Birches Lane
Coventry
A46
A452
½ mile

Kenilworth Common
OS SHEET 140; SP 297 730

LOCATION On the northern side of Kenilworth, the reserve is situated on Common Lane off either the A429 or Dalehouse Lane.

P Parking on Forge Road, Woodmill Meadow, Highland Road and Woodland Road.

Coventry + bus to Kenilworth (bus stops outside reserve .

GETTING AROUND

SIZE 11.8 ha (29.2 acres)
Flat in parts, muddy in winter, various entrance gates, numerous paths

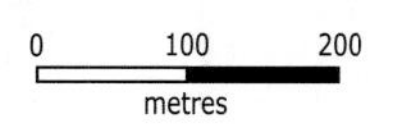

Fritillary

Leam Valley

This beautiful and diverse LNR includes a delightful stretch of the meandering River Leam, with its grassy margins, marshland, woodlands, ponds and a lake

Best time to visit

WINTER ✔

BIRDS Ducks including tufted duck (BELOW), geese, waders, finches, tits

SPRING ✔

PLANTS Cowslip, fritillary, willows, marsh-marigold, cuckooflower (BELOW), yellow iris
BIRDS Skylark, kestrel, warblers, little ringed plover

SUMMER ✔

PLANTS Yellow water-lily, ragged-robin, purple-loosestrife, flowering-rush
INSECTS Damselflies and dragonflies, butterflies
REPTILES Grass snake (BELOW)
BIRDS Kingfisher

AUTUMN ✔

BIRDS Barn owl (BELOW)

The River Leam holds numerous fish with roach, perch and common bream lurking in its depths. A magnificent range of dragonflies and damselflies flit along its banks including banded demoiselle, darters, chasers, hawkers and the emperor dragonfly.

Kingfishers favour this site and are known to breed along the river, offering regular viewings. Even the elusive grass snake may be seen as it swims amongst arrowhead, yellow water-lilies and flowering-rush.

The river margins present marsh-marigold, yellow iris and purple-loosestrife alongside rushes, sweet-grass and common reed and there is an area of uncommon greater tussock-sedge. It is hoped that one day soon, this ideal habitat will welcome the arrival of otter as it gradually recolonises the county.

The rich marsh is dense with many marsh-loving plants, including cuckooflower, ragged-robin and even rare fritillary.

Over the largest area of grassland, cowslips are charmingly scattered amongst the many species of grasses. An abundance of butterflies are attracted including brimstone, peacock, comma and red admiral, with plenty of browns, whites and skippers.

Skylark breed here, and the magical barn owl and kestrel can be seen hunting for small mammals hiding in the long grass.

Excavated in 2000, the wetland supports further bird life with gatherings of ducks, geese and occasional waders such as little ringed plover and snipe which can be viewed from the hide. A number of small, spring-fed ponds provide ideal habitat for both common frog and newts which relish their shady waters, breeding year on year.

... continued overleaf ▶

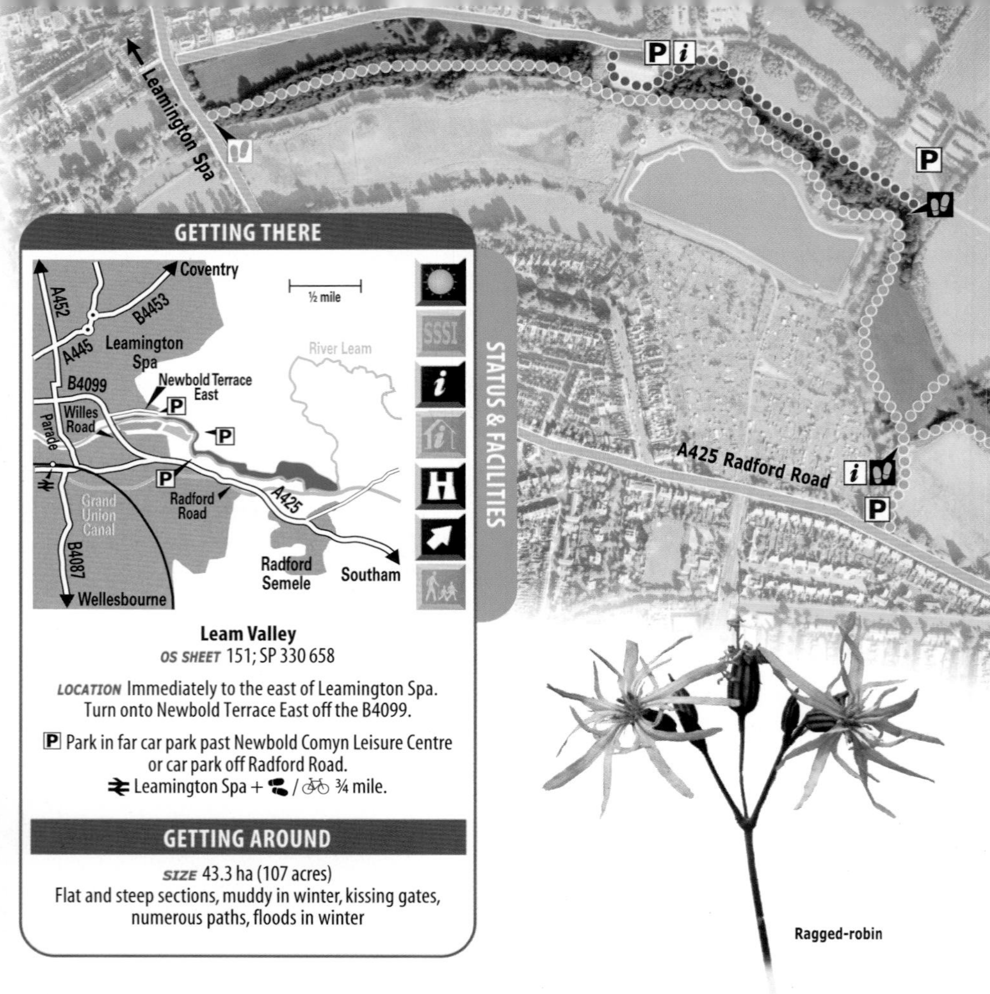

Ragged-robin

The woodland, planted since the 1970s, has good specimens of oak, ash and field maple and a few examples of unusual almond and purple willow can be discovered. Finches, tits and warblers are numerous, with splendid jay, sparrowhawk and even the shy woodcock in winter.

Delightfully, signs of badger activity are obvious around the reserve – their routes clearly defined from regular foraging trips. Red fox also hunts here, rewarded with rich pickings from the banquet of small rodents, insects and amphibians which prosper.

Fungi appear in the autumn with chicken-of-the-wood possibly sprouting on an oak tree, shaggy bracket on ash and the rare willow bracket on fallen crack willows at the west end of the reserve. Smaller ground mushrooms are frequent and fairy rings can be spotted in several places on mown grass.

Adjoining the reserve is the rest of Newbold Comyn Park with small patches of woodland, hedgerow, rough grassland and recreational grounds, all offering opportunities for walking, exploration and seeing additional wildlife.

Welches Meadow reserve is just across the river and a closed hibernaculum for bats is monitored by the Trust near the reservoir, where they can be viewed as they feed over the water.

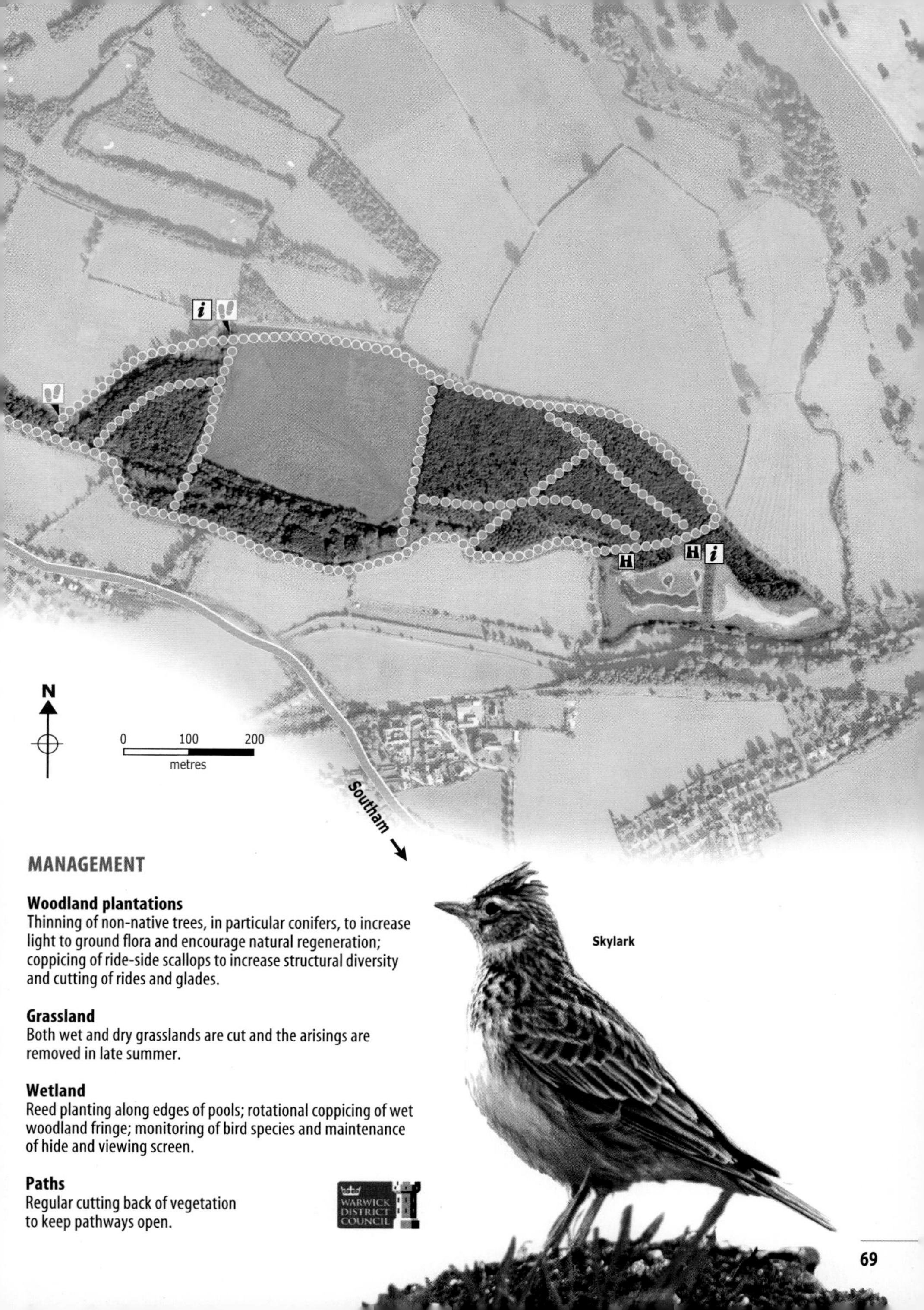

MANAGEMENT

Woodland plantations
Thinning of non-native trees, in particular conifers, to increase light to ground flora and encourage natural regeneration; coppicing of ride-side scallops to increase structural diversity and cutting of rides and glades.

Grassland
Both wet and dry grasslands are cut and the arisings are removed in late summer.

Wetland
Reed planting along edges of pools; rotational coppicing of wet woodland fringe; monitoring of bird species and maintenance of hide and viewing screen.

Paths
Regular cutting back of vegetation to keep pathways open.

Cowslip

Loxley Church Meadow

This ancient and unimproved species-rich hay meadow is one of the richest cowslip meadows in the county

Best time to visit

SPRING ✔

PLANTS Cowslip, meadow foxtail (BELOW), ancient hedges
INSECTS Orange-tip butterfly

SUMMER ✔

PLANTS Oxeye daisy, rough hawkbit, common spotted-orchid, yellow rattle, dropwort, grasses
INSECTS Common blue, small copper and ringlet (BELOW) butterflies

AUTUMN ✔

PLANTS Hedgerow fruits including sloes (BELOW)

WINTER

Formed on slightly calcareous to neutral soil, the site has prospered over ancient ridge and furrow. Its old hedgerows, tall trees and ambling stream offer diversity worthy of its SSSI designation.

Over 120 flower species flourish at this delightful reserve, providing an array of colour, including oxeye daisy, yellow rattle, common spotted-orchid and rough hawkbit. Twenty-three species of grass have been identified, with crested dog's-tail, sweet vernal-grass and false oat-grass common place.

Twenty-two butterfly species can be found in this pleasant meadow, with orange-tip, common blue and small copper all frequent.

Hedgerows hint towards an ancient history dating back some 600 years. Ash, oak, field maple and suckering English elm are present, with many shrubs including hawthorn, dogwood, hazel and wild privet offering cover to a variety of birds and small mammals.

MANAGEMENT

Loxley Church Meadow is managed as a traditional hay meadow by taking a hay crop in July and grazing during autumn.

GETTING THERE

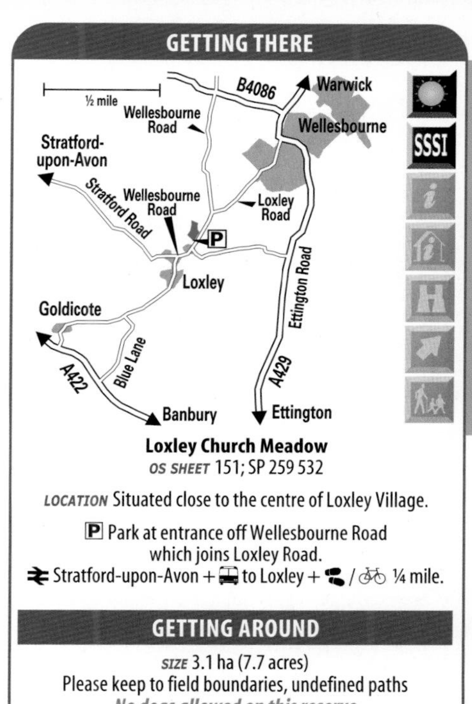

Loxley Church Meadow
OS SHEET 151; SP 259 532

LOCATION Situated close to the centre of Loxley Village.

P Park at entrance off Wellesbourne Road which joins Loxley Road.

Stratford-upon-Avon + bus to Loxley + walk / cycle ¼ mile.

GETTING AROUND

SIZE 3.1 ha (7.7 acres)

Please keep to field boundaries, undefined paths

No dogs allowed on this reserve

Common blue

White-clawed crayfish

Newbold Quarry

This popular disused quarry offers calcareous grassland, woodland and an excellent lake, all deserving of its LNR protection

Best time to visit

WINTER ✔

BIRDS Pochard (BELOW), tufted duck, teal, little grebe

SPRING ✔

PLANTS Wild strawberry (BELOW), twayblade
BIRDS Spring migrants, songbirds, coot, great crested grebe

SUMMER ✔

PLANTS Bee orchid, common spotted-orchid, blue fleabane, lesser bulrush
INSECTS Brown hawker dragonfly (BELOW)
AMPHIBIANS Common toad

AUTUMN ✔

PLANTS Carline thistle (BELOW)

Blue lias rock was quarried here for the local cement industry until 1920, when natural springs flooded the pit. Now the deep lake is the predominant feature at this reserve and is vitally important for its thriving population of native white-clawed crayfish, as well as being a significant breeding site for many thousands of toads in spring.

Aquatic plants such as curly waterweed, spiked water-milfoil and lesser bulrush provide coverage to breeding great crested grebe and coot, with the lake welcoming tufted duck, pochard and little grebe in colder months.

The lime-rich, clay spoil heaps support characteristic flowers including wild strawberry and bird's-foot-trefoil, with twayblade, common spotted-orchid and bee orchid. There is also a good selection of butterflies.

The hawthorn scrub grades into woodland of ash and sycamore, where a wonderful variety of songbirds congregate including an assortment of finches, tits and warblers.

MANAGEMENT

Management focuses on scrub removal on the banks surrounding the lake, reed planting and coppicing of the willows along the water's edge.

RUGBY

GETTING THERE

Newbold Quarry
OS SHEET 140; SP 497 770

LOCATION Located at Newbold on Avon, north west of Rugby.

P Car parks can be accessed off the A426, via Yates Avenue or for RADAR key holders off the B4112 Newbold Road.
Rugby + bus to Newbold on Avon + walk / cycle ½ mile.

GETTING AROUND

SIZE 10.5 ha (26 acres)
Part of the reserve has wheelchair access, steep slopes in parts

STATUS & FACILITIES

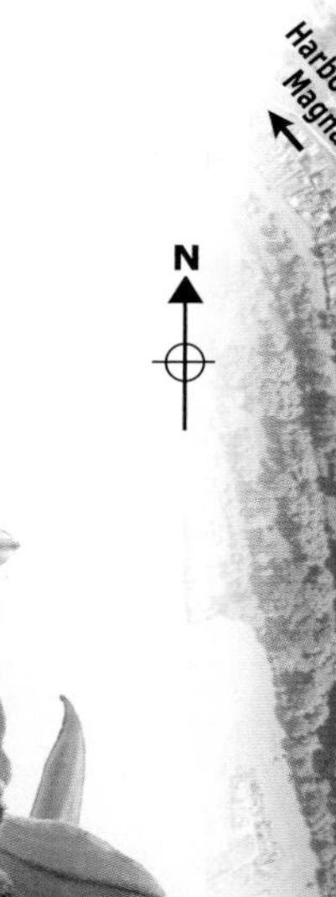

Bee orchid

Opposite-leaved golden-saxifrage

Radway Meadows

Beneath the wooded scarp slope of Edge Hill, these two species-rich acidic meadows have a wet flush, stream and ancient hedgerows

Best time to visit

SPRING ✔

PLANTS Opposite-leaved golden-saxifrage, Midland hawthorn, adder's-tongue, sweet vernal-grass
BIRDS Skylark (BELOW)

SUMMER ✔

PLANTS Betony (BELOW), dropwort, ragged-robin, goat's-beard, water figwort, dog-rose, field rose, grasses

AUTUMN ✔

PLANTS Hedgerow colour and fruit including Midland hawthorn (BELOW)

WINTER

These sloping fields sit in an historic Civil War landscape alongside an ancient hollow way which is also a parish boundary.

Occupying a magnificent setting, this delightful reserve is situated at the north-eastern tip of the Cotswolds Area of Outstanding Natural Beauty, the only AONB in Warwickshire.

Lying over ancient ridge and furrow, the meadows offer uncommon betony, dropwort and adder's-tongue, with grasses such as crested dog's-tail and sweet vernal-grass. Wetter areas suit a variety of damp loving plants including opposite-leaved golden-saxifrage, ragged-robin, water figwort and goat's-beard.

The sumptuous hedgerows suggest an age of at least 400 years and contain oak, ash, English elm, crab apple and pear, with crack and white willows, and the occasional midland hawthorn amongst many others. Dog-rose and field rose scramble through the tangle producing pretty flowers in summer months and ripe hips, adding dashes of colour in the autumn.

GETTING THERE

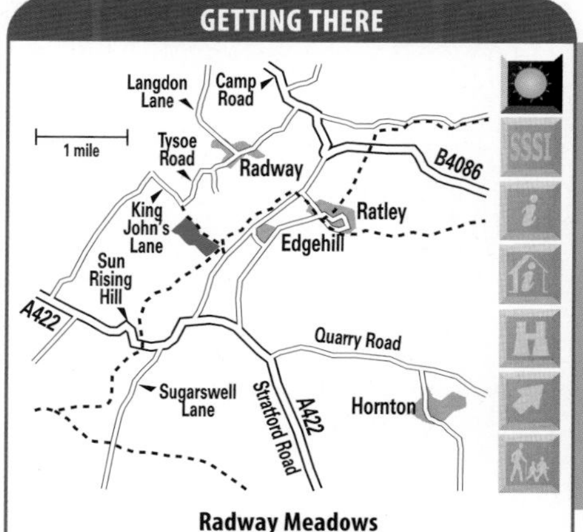

STATUS & FACILITIES

SSSI

Radway Meadows
OS SHEET 151; SP 366 475

LOCATION Situated near the village of Radway, south of Kineton. Access and off road parking on King John's Lane.

P Off road parking on King John's Lane.
Banbury or Stratford + bus to Radway + walk / cycle 1 mile.

GETTING AROUND

SIZE 9.4 ha (23 acres)
Gentle slopes, undefined paths, soft patches, muddy in winter

MANAGEMENT

The meadows are grazed by both cattle and sheep.

Treecreeper

Rough Hill Wood

Forming part of the Wirehill Wood SSSI, Rough Hill Wood is situated on the county border with Worcestershire. This truly ancient woodland can be traced as far back as 1250

Best time to visit

WINTER ✔
PLANTS Holly (BELOW)

SPRING ✔
PLANTS Bluebell, bilberry, wood anemone, small-leaved and large leaved lime, wild service-tree, primrose
BIRDS Jay, treecreeper, cuckoo, lesser spotted woodpecker (BELOW)

SUMMER ✔
PLANTS Heather, betony, foxglove, broad-leaved helleborine (BELOW)
INSECTS Brimstone, white admiral, gatekeeper and small tortoiseshell butterflies

AUTUMN ✔
FUNGI Woodland fungi including horn-of-plenty (BELOW)
PLANTS Bilberry fruit

Dominating the hillside along 'the Slough', this splendid woodland reserve is teeming with diversity, its mixed geology giving rise to distinct woodland types.

Although sessile oak is prevalent, the wood also offers birch, rowan, aspen and small-leaved lime. Even its cousin the large-leaved lime can be found. An understorey of hazel and midland hawthorn competes with holly and wild privet.

Bluebell, wood anemone and primrose celebrate spring and provide a blanket of vibrant colour to the dappled woodland floor. Uncommon bilberry, heather, broad-leaved helleborine and betony also grace these woods with their presence.

Autumn visits are rewarded with an extensive range of fungi that can be found growing under the strikingly colourful woodland canopy.

Notable for its birds, Rough Hill Wood boasts cuckoo, all three woodpecker species, chiffchaff and long-tailed tit, together with an abundance of other woodland and song birds.

MANAGEMENT

Management focuses on rotational coppicing of the lower slopes of the woodland and maintaining a small area of heathland.

GETTING THERE

Rough Hill Wood

OS SHEET 150; SP 052 637

LOCATION Just north-west of Studley, near Redditch. The reserve can be accessed off the A448, The Slough.

P Park at reserve entrance on the A448.

Redditch + No. 518 to the Slough close to reserve entrance.

GETTING AROUND

SIZE 21 ha (52 acres)

Steep slopes, wet and muddy patches in winter

STATUS & FACILITIES

SSSI

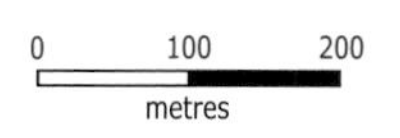

Wood anemone

Herb-Paris

Snitterfield Bushes

With its grassy rides and glades, ponds, ditches and wet flushes, this tranquil damp woodland of ash and oak offers splendid diversity

Best time to visit

WINTER ✓

BIRDS Woodcock
MAMMALS Muntjac, roe (BELOW) and fallow deer

SPRING ✓

FUNGI Semifree morel (BELOW)
PLANTS Early-purple orchid, bird's-nest orchid, bluebell, primrose, herb-Paris
INSECTS Grizzled skipper butterfly
BIRDS Warblers, bullfinch

SUMMER ✓

PLANTS Caucasian stonecrop, columbine, fragrant agrimony (BELOW)
INSECTS White admiral, silver-washed fritillary, marbled white and white-letter hairstreak butterflies, glow-worm

AUTUMN ✓

FUNGI Boletes, milkcaps, bonnets and puffballs
PLANTS Meadow saffron
BIRDS Jay (BELOW)

Situated just north of Shakespeare's historic Stratford-Upon-Avon, Snitterfield Bushes reserve lies either side of the Snitterfield to Bearley Road, and once formed part of a much larger area of semi-natural, broad-leaved woodland.

Natural forest for centuries, the wood was used for timber, common pasture and agriculture, and ridge and furrow plough markings are still evident in some areas of the reserve. The site was utilised as an airfield during the 2nd World War and traces of the old concrete runway network and bomb stores can be found towards the centre of the reserve.

Following clear-felling of the woodland in the 1940s, the site has now been returned to its current excellence through careful management, and is certainly deserving of its SSSI status.

Lying on lime rich clay soils, the woodland is predominantly oak, ash, silver birch and field maple. Below its even-aged canopy, a shrub layer of wild privet, wayfaring-tree, dogwood and midland hawthorn form a jumbled understorey. A mature specimen of wych elm can be found here – now a rarity n the county following an epidemic of Dutch elm disease which destroyed many of the trees in the 1970s and 1980s.

Surrendering to an exquisite carpet of bluebells, primroses and early-purple orchids during spring time, the woodland supports a further 250 species of plants, including a number of more special flowers, found at limited sites across Warwickshire, such as herb-paris, fragrant agrimony, columbine, meadow saffron and bird's-nest orchid.

Autumn brings an impressive selection of fungi including boletes, milkcaps, bonnets and puffballs galore.

... continued overleaf ▶

Common puffball

Sixty species of bird have been recorded here with woodcock warranting a winter visit and turtle dove and many warblers in the spring. The colourful jay can be seen burying acorns in the autumn, the forgotten seeds giving rise to many oak saplings in the coming warmer months.

The reserve also boasts excellent lists of insects, including 28 species of butterfly, notably white-letter hairstreak, marbled white, grizzled skipper and silver-washed fritillary. A total of 260 species of macromoth have been recorded and 89 species of hoverfly. Beetles relish these woods with 177 species recorded, including glow-worm which is known to breed here.

Roe and fallow deer frequent the woods, and can occasionally be seen feeding quietly amongst the trees. Badger and fox afford a very rare sighting, but are regular visitors to this tremendous reserve.

MANAGEMENT

Woodland
Traditional management of rotational coppicing with standards; dead wood habitat piles created from brash

Rides and glades
Network of rides and woodland glades are cut on rotation in late summer / early autumn

Ponds
Scrub coppiced around the edges of ponds to prevent encroachment and excessive shading of the water

Bird and bat boxes
Monitored on a regular basis

Marbled white

Spring flowers at Snitterfield Bushes: early-purple orchids, primroses and germander speedwell

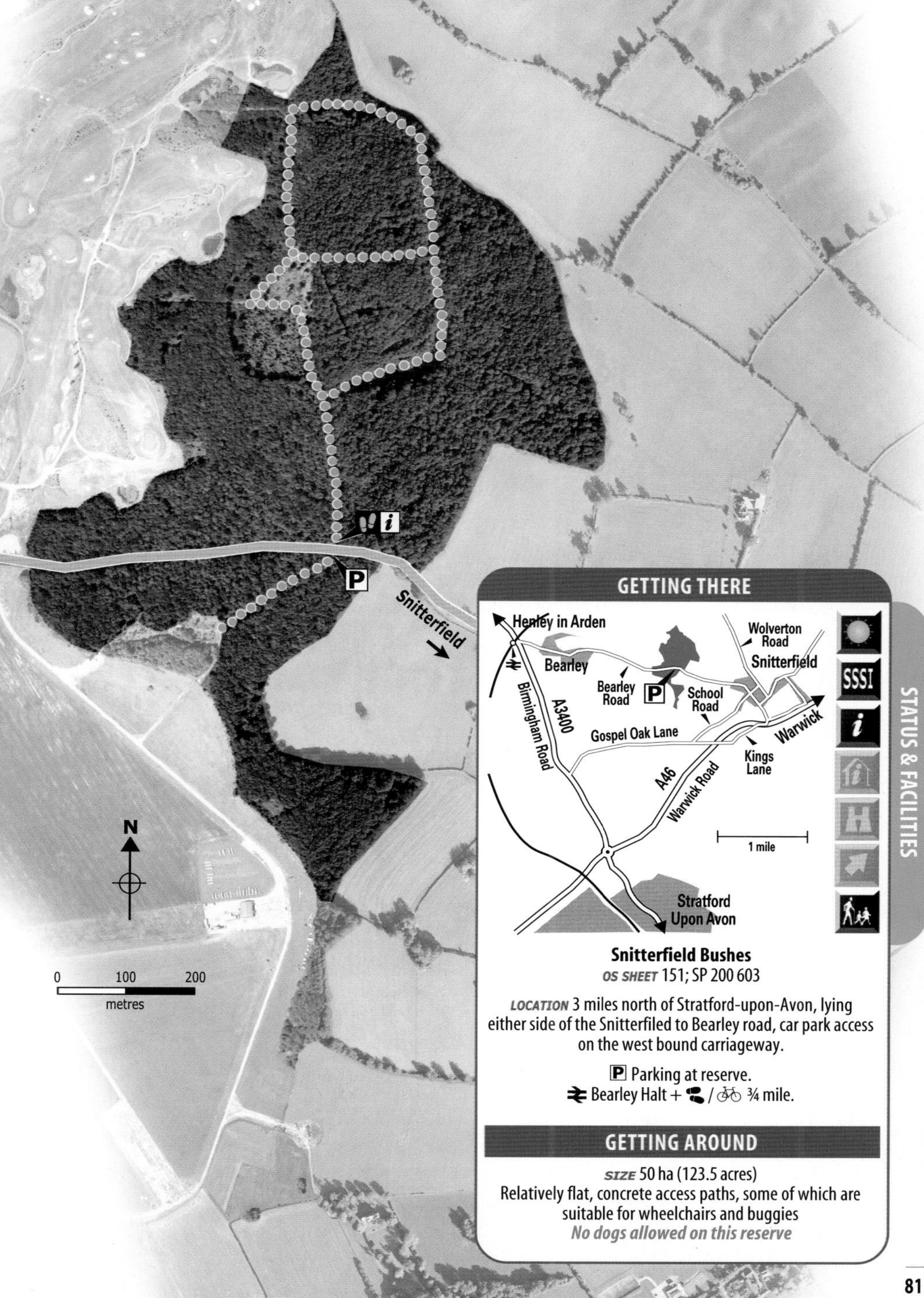

GETTING THERE

Snitterfield Bushes

OS SHEET 151; SP 200 603

LOCATION 3 miles north of Stratford-upon-Avon, lying either side of the Snitterfiled to Bearley road, car park access on the west bound carriageway.

P Parking at reserve.

Bearley Halt + / ¾ mile.

GETTING AROUND

SIZE 50 ha (123.5 acres)

Relatively flat, concrete access paths, some of which are suitable for wheelchairs and buggies

No dogs allowed on this reserve

Green tiger beetle

Stockton Cutting

Established as a reserve in 1977, this redundant railway cutting and abandoned quarry have been transformed into a species-rich SSSI, its grassland, woodland, scrub and pool creating a diverse haven for wildlife

Best time to visit

WINTER ✔

PLANTS Spurge-laurel (BELOW)
BIRDS Siskin, redpoll
MAMMALS Muntjac

SPRING ✔

PLANTS Hairy violet, false oxlip
INSECTS Green tiger beetle, green hairstreak and holly blue (BELOW) butterflies
REPTILES Grass snake
BIRDS Warblers

SUMMER ✔

PLANTS Greater butterfly-orchid (BELOW), common spotted-orchid, dwarf thistle, woolly thistle, blue fleabane, wild thyme
INSECTS Common blue and marbled white butterflies
BIRDS Green woodpecker

AUTUMN ✔

PLANTS Carline thistle, autumn gentian, shrub fruits including buckthorn (BELOW)

Steep banks of hawthorn, ash, field maple and wild cherry tangle with wild privet, buckthorn and even the rare spurge-laurel, to create a refuge for over 30 species of birds.

The woodland of predominantly ash and sycamore provides good sighting opportunities for all three species of woodpecker and even woodcock.

Calcareous grassland hides less common plants like hairy violet, false oxlip, dwarf thistle, autumn gentian, wild thyme and the scarce blue fleabane. Twayblade, common spotted-orchid and greater butterfly-orchid appear and are well worth a visit.

Thirty-two butterfly species have been recorded including green hairstreak, marbled white, holly blue and common blue. The scarce brilliant green tiger beetle can often be seen running on the short grassland in May.

Grass snakes, rabbit and muntjac are all visitors to this pleasant reserve, with intermittent signs of the elusive badger.

MANAGEMENT

Management involves an annual grass cut in the bottom of the cutting and clearing scrub from the sides of the cutting.

GETTING THERE

Princethorpe
Rugby
Long Itchington
Grand Union Canal
Cuttle
Stockton Road
Napton Road
Station Road
A423
A426
Stockton
1 mile
Banbury

SSSI

STATUS & FACILITIES

Stockton Cutting

OS SHEET 151; SP 437 651

LOCATION North-east of Southam, 1 km north of Stockton on the Napton Road. From the A423 take the A426 towards Rugby. The reserve is approximately ¾ mile on the right, after the turning for Napton Road.

P Park on the verge at reserve entrance.
Leamington Spa + No. 63 to Stockton + / ¾ mile.

GETTING AROUND

SIZE 5.5 ha (13.6 acres)

Generally flat but with some steep, sloped areas with steps, muddy in winter. Stile at entrance.

Noctule bat

Stonebridge Meadows

Perched on the southern edge of Coventry, sandwiched between the A45 and the River Sowe, Stonebridge Meadows are a relict of an earlier agricultural landscape

Best time to visit

WINTER ✔

BIRDS Fieldfare (BELOW), redwing, buzzard

SPRING ✔

PLANTS Alder wood, marsh-marigold (BELOW), bluebell

SUMMER ✔

PLANTS Harebell (BELOW), betony, lesser spearwort, skullcap, willowherbs
INSECTS Dragonflies, butterflies
MAMMALS Bats

AUTUMN ✔

FUNGI Horse mushroom (BELOW)

This Local Nature Reserve occupies a southerly aspect within the Sowe Valley and joins the neighbouring reserves of Stoke Floods and Wyken Slough in forming a vital part of the Sowe Valley 'Green Corridor'.

The site presents an interesting mix of habitats, with a combination of acidic and neutral grassland, with marshy areas prevalent on the lower lying ground. Grazed for the last 150 years, Stonebridge Meadows harbours many wild flowers including locally uncommon harebell, with damper areas revealing a medley of marsh-loving species including willowherbs and bulrush.

A summer's day offers the chance to see many butterfly and other insect species. Over 260 species of beetle have been recorded here, and several dragonflies too. Early evenings provide a veritable banquet of insects for noctule and long-eared bats.

An alder wood planted in the 1850s for the local clog industry now supports a multitude of life under its canopy, whilst the dense hawthorn, gorse and broom which occupies the western end of the reserve attracts many song birds including resident and migrant thrushes.

MANAGEMENT

Highland cattle are grazed year round to manage the grassland and pockets of alder woodland are managed by coppicing.

GETTING THERE

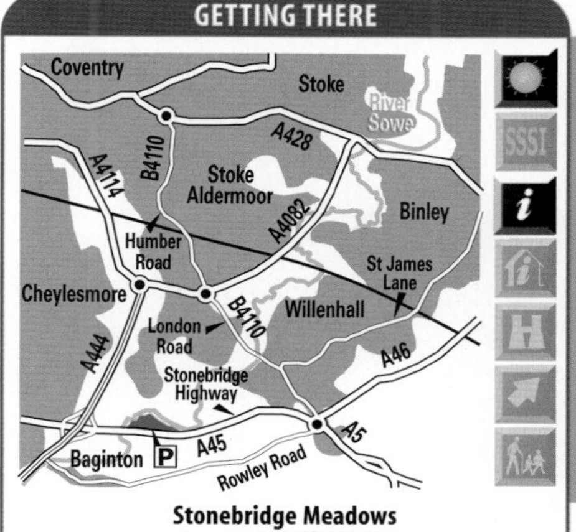

STATUS & FACILITIES

Stonebridge Meadows
OS SHEET 140; SP 348 756

LOCATION On the southern edge of Coventry, situated off the A45 Stonebridge Highway (east bound carriage way), adjacent to Jaguar's Whitley Plant.

P Park in lay-by on the east-bound A45.
Coventry + bus to Stonebridge Island + walk / cycle ¼ mile.

GETTING AROUND

SIZE 7.7 ha (19 acres)
Informal paths can become wet and muddy. Gentle slopes, some floods in winter. Entrance over stile.

0 100 200
metres

N

Coventry City Council

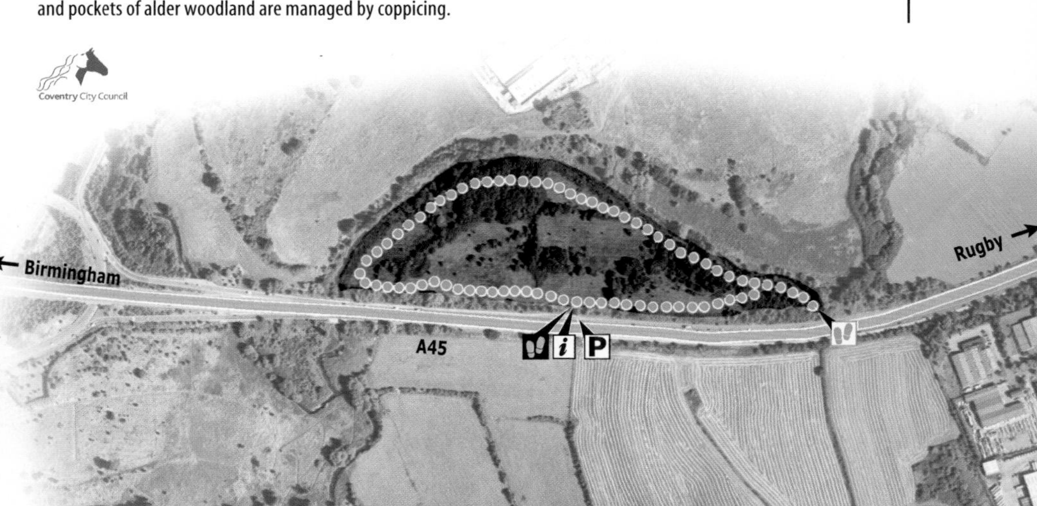

Beefsteak fungus

Tocil Wood and Meadow

Designated a Local Nature Reserve, this delightful ancient wood and meadow is now enveloped by the University of Warwick campus

Best time to visit

SPRING ✔

PLANTS Wood anemone, marsh-marigold, buttercups, large bittercress, violets, dog's mercury, wood-sorrel (BELOW), bluebell
AMPHIBIANS Toad
BIRDS Warblers

SUMMER ✔

PLANTS Meadowsweet, great willowherb (BELOW)
MAMMALS Bats, stoat, weasel

AUTUMN ✔

FUNGI Beefsteak fungus, stinkhorn, buttercap
PLANTS Hart's-tongue fern (BELOW)

WINTER

Lying on Liassic sandstone and Triassic clay, this pleasurable reserve contains three main habitats – oak woodland, swamp and a wet meadow.

Named Towsall Grove in 1588, this site's antiquity is illustrated by 1st and 2nd century earthworks in the south, with ridge and furrow confirming medieval agriculture. Indeed, historical evidence shows the wood to be at least 400 years old.

Under a canopy of oak, sycamore and ash, hazel, elder and rowan create a shady woodland floor where bluebells abound. Dog's mercury, wood-sorrel, wood anemone and violets offer springtime gems. Autumn brings an array of colour and the intriguing beefsteak fungus, stinkhorn and buttercap.

The wetland sustains alder and goat willow, sedges and rush, with dashes of colour from marsh-marigold and the uncommon large bittercress. Hart's-tongue fern can be found along the bank of the stream.

In the spring the meadow is beautiful with cuckooflower, buttercups and meadowsweet, all attracting an abundance of insects, which in turn provide a feeding ground for many species of bat.

The reserve is good for migrant warblers and over 60 species of birds have been recorded. Even the shy stoat and weasel occasionally afford the discerning visitor a rare treat.

MANAGEMENT

Management focuses on cutting one third of the meadow each year in the summer and rotational coppicing in the woodland through the winter.

Coventry City Council

GETTING THERE

Kirby Corner Road, University of Warwick, Gibbet Hill Road, Coventry, A429, A45, A46, St. Martin's Road, Finham, Gibbet Hill, River Sowe, 1 mile, Crackley, Stoneleigh Road, Coventry Road, Stoneleigh, Dalehouse Lane, B4115, Kenilworth, Stoneleigh Road

Tocil Wood and Meadow

OS SHEET 140; SP 304 754

LOCATION On the southern edge of Coventry, situated in the University of Warwick Campus. The reserve can be accessed from Gibbet Hill Road off the A429 Kenilworth Road.

P Roadside parking off Gibbet Hill.
Coventry + bus to University of Warwick campus or Gibbet Hill + walk / cycle ½ mile.

GETTING AROUND

SIZE 5.8 ha (14.3 acres)
Relatively flat paths, can be muddy

STATUS & FACILITIES
SSSI

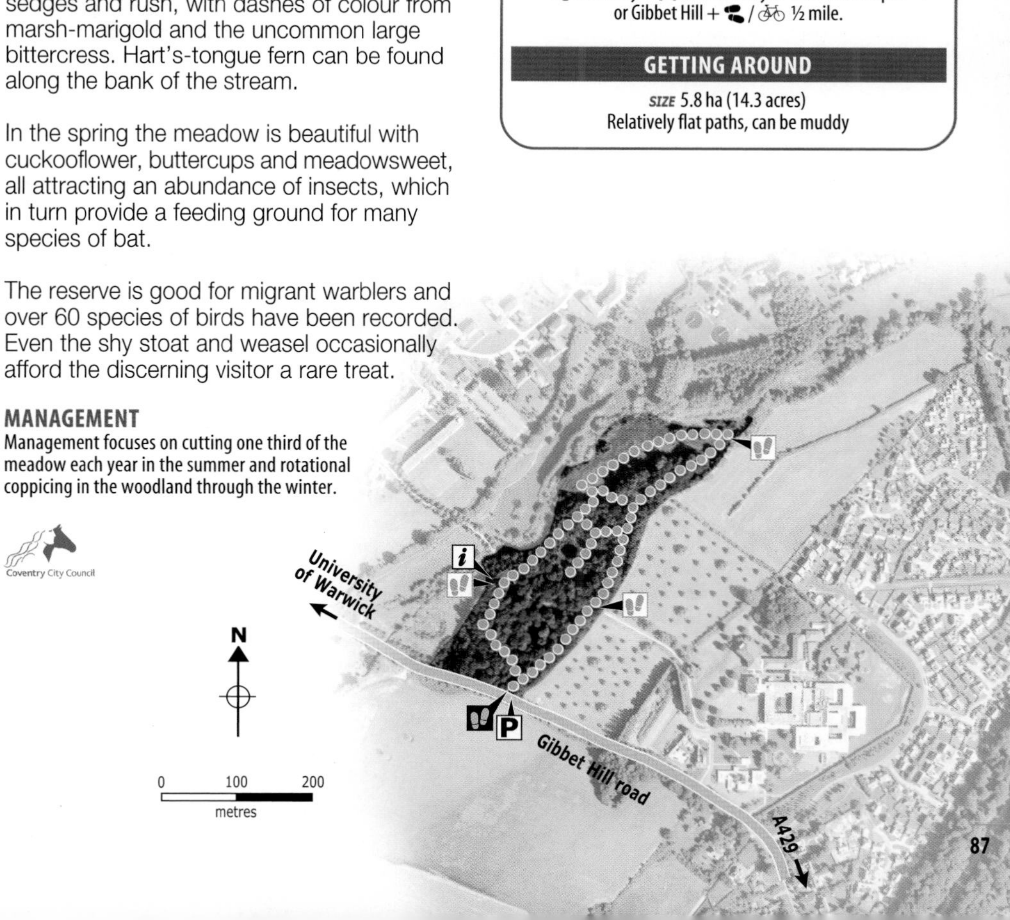

Silverweed

Welches Meadow

This traditional flood meadow provides seasonal shallow water, damp grassland, marsh, trees and shrubs. Situated close to the centre of Leamington Spa, the area was created for flood defence in the 1840s

Best time to visit

WINTER ✔

BIRDS Canada geese, teal (BELOW), snipe, gulls

SPRING ✔

PLANTS Yellow iris
INSECTS Orange-tip (BELOW) and holly blue butterflies
BIRDS Grey heron

SUMMER ✔

PLANTS Marsh bedstraw, silverweed, yellowcresses, wild angelica
INSECTS Dragonflies and damselflies including banded demoiselle (BELOW) and white-legged damselfly
REPTILES Grass snake

AUTUMN

Bounded by the meandering River Leam, Willes Road, housing and a reservoir, this popular LNR feels surprisingly secluded.

The damp meadow has many wild flowers with yellowcresses, marsh bedstraw and silverweed all plentiful. The eastern marsh has reed sweet-grass and reed canary-grass intermingled with yellow iris, greater pond-sedge and wild angelica.

Its boundaries include oak, ash, willow and hawthorn with ivy, dog-rose and bramble. Common lime, horse-chestnut and beech occur towards the housing, with Turkey oak and wild cherry flanking the road.

The reserve hides a wide diversity of insects including some notable beetle species. Butterflies are abundant with holly blue, orange-tip and small heath present. Brown hawker dragonflies, banded demoiselle and white-legged damselfly flit across the meadow and along the river banks.

When flooded, flocks of gulls and Canada geese congregate here with mallard and teal. The hunched grey heron provides regular viewing as it fishes in the river's shallows.

MANAGEMENT

The meadow is cut each summer and the cut sward is removed. Further management entails the removal of willow saplings and encroaching scrub.

WARWICK DISTRICT COUNCIL

GETTING THERE

STATUS & FACILITIES

Welches Meadow
OS SHEET 151; SP 325 657

LOCATION Close to the centre of Leamington Spa, access to the meadow can be gained from the B4099, Willes Road.

P Roadside parking in Willes Road.
Leamington Spa + / ¾ mile.

GETTING AROUND

SIZE 6.7 ha (16.6 acres)
Flat, informal paths, floods in winter.
Please keep to field boundaries

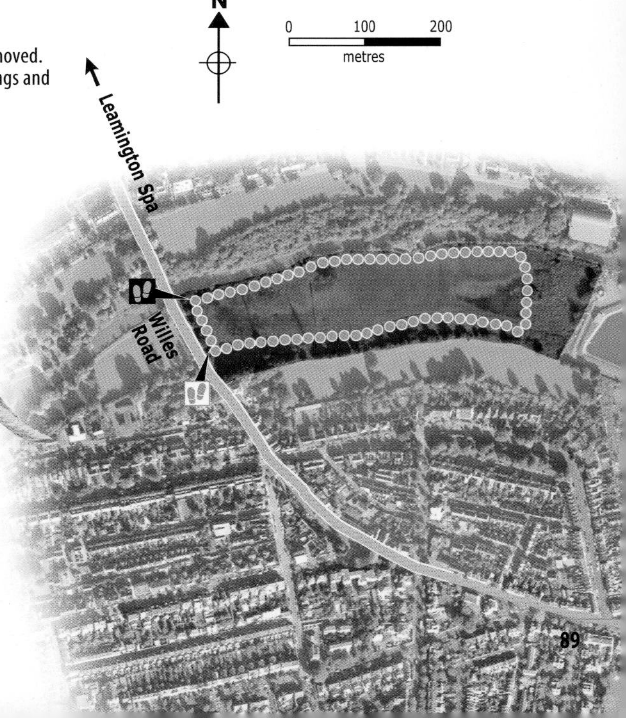

Yellow iris

Woolly thistle

Welcombe Hills

Offering distant views across the traditional landscape of the Avon, this splendid undulating LNR offers rich and varied wildlife. Lying on the edge of the historic town of Stratford-upon-Avon, the reserve once formed part of the formal grounds to Sir John Clopton's residence, Clopton House

Best time to visit

SPRING ✔

PLANTS Adder's-tongue
BIRDS Raven, buzzard, sparrowhawk, kestrel (BELOW), treecreeper, green and great spotted woodpeckers, finches

SUMMER ✔

PLANTS Woolly thistle, quaking-grass (BELOW),
BIRDS Little owl

AUTUMN ✔

INSECTS Comma butterfly (BELOW)

WINTER

Welcombe Hills reserve may have got its name from the historically important well found at the site which is inscribed 'SJC 1686'. Margaret, daughter of William Clopton who died in 1592 supposedly drowned here. It was around this time that Shakespeare was writing his famous play Hamlet and it is believed that this tragic event provided inspiration for his 'Ophelia' and her lonely death.

Welcombe Hills now provides delightful walks through grassland and woodland. Woolly thistle, quaking-grass and adder's-tongue hide yellow meadow ant hills which illustrate the wonderful lack of disturbance. The woodland is full of oak, horse-chestnut and beech with English elm.

Birds are plentiful, with great spotted woodpecker, sparrowhawk, little owl, treecreeper and finches enjoying the woodland where ravens breed in spring.

GETTING THERE

STATUS & FACILITIES

Welcombe Hills
OS SHEET 150; SP 205 565

LOCATION Close to the centre of Stratford-upon-Avon. Turn off the A439 Warwick Road onto Ingon Lane.

P Parking available on Maidenhead Road, off Ingon Lane.
Stratford-upon-Avon + / 1½ miles.

GETTING AROUND

SIZE 60 ha (148 acres)
Steep slopes in parts, access via kissing gates.
Stunning views.

N

0 100 200
metres

Stratford-upon-Avon

MANAGEMENT

Management focuses on removing most of the hawthorn scrub in 'keeper's field' – the area of the site which is botanically richest. Cattle graze the majority of the rest of the nature reserve.

Water mint

Alvecote Meadows

Forming part of Warwickshire's largest SSSI, this wetland reserve comprises two delightful meadows, swampland and a small stream

The meadow's rough grassland supports creeping buttercup, sedges and rushes, giving way to soft rush as it invades the wetter west meadow. Greater pond-sedge, reed canary-grass and reed sweet-grass crowd the swamp, with lesser water-parsnip, water mint and common fleabane representing some of the more interesting flowers to be seen.

Twenty-four species of butterfly have been recorded here, including dingy skipper, small heath and wall brown all making appearances. Marshy areas provide habitat for several nationally scarce beetles. Ruddy darter dragonflies are a familiar sight darting by the stream that divides the two meadows, and even the occasional common hawker, a rarity in Warwickshire, may be seen.

Alvecote Meadow's mature oaks, ash and willow offer ideal roosting spots to tawny owl, sparrowhawk and an array of finches. The grassland attracts snipe, lapwing and little egret. Grass snake, frog, toad and newts are regular visitors to this reserve.

MANAGEMENT

The management of this reserve entails taking a haycut from the dry meadow during the summer followed by aftermath grazing using Highland cattle. The wet meadow is grazed all year round.

GETTING THERE

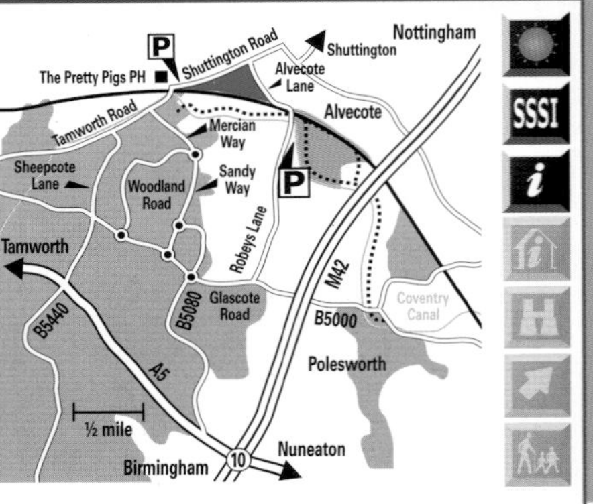

SSSI

STATUS & FACILITIES

Alvecote Meadows
OS SHEET 139; SK 245 048

LOCATION Just north east of Tamworth, situated on Robeys Lane and Shuttington Road. There is a path link from the entrance nearest the Pretty Pigs Pub, which leads through the reserve and towards Alvecote village.

P Pretty Pigs Pub car park or roadside off Alvecote Lane.
Tamworth station + bus to Shuttington (stops at end of Alvecote Lane).

GETTING AROUND

SIZE 11.3 ha (28 acres)
Flat, but no wheelchair access as soft patches.
Floods in winter, stiles
No dogs allowed on this reserve

Best time to visit

WINTER ✔
BIRDS Canada goose, mute swan, heron

SPRING ✔
AMPHIBIANS Frogs and toads
BIRDS Little egret

SUMMER ✔
PLANTS Sedges and rushes, golden dock, water mint
INSECTS Dragonflies and damselflies, butterflies
REPTILES Grass snake

AUTUMN ✔
PLANTS Hawthorn berries
BIRDS Snipe, plover

Guelder-rose fruits

Cock Robin Wood

Although only planted in 1989, this small, attractive woodland is already forming an interesting and diverse area for wildlife

Created on arable farmland on the edge of Rugby, this reserve was created on land donated by Sainsbury's, to mitigate the building of its nearby supermarket.

The diverse mixture of habitats that have developed now support an already impressive array of plants and animals.

A large pool adds considerable diversity, with water-lilies and pondweeds hiding an assortment of aquatic life. Frog, toad, moorhen and dragonfly breed here, with fascinating water boatmen and diving beetles indicating the successful creation of the fast-establishing pool.

MANAGEMENT

Management involves maintaining the open grassy glades and cutting back the ride edges.

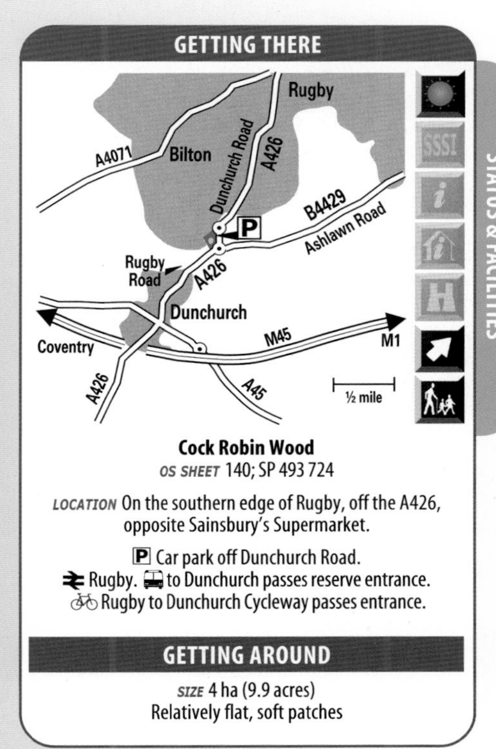

Cock Robin Wood

OS SHEET 140; SP 493 724

LOCATION On the southern edge of Rugby, off the A426, opposite Sainsbury's Supermarket.

P Car park off Dunchurch Road.

Rugby. to Dunchurch passes reserve entrance.

Rugby to Dunchurch Cycleway passes entrance.

GETTING AROUND

SIZE 4 ha (9.9 acres)

Relatively flat, soft patches

Best time to visit

WINTER	SPRING ✔	SUMMER ✔	AUTUMN ✔
	AMPHIBIANS Frogs and toads	*PLANTS* Shrub flowers *INSECTS* Pond life, dragonflies	*PLANTS* Shrub fruits, leaf colour

Deans Green

This peaceful reserve comprises two traditional hay meadows bounded by species-rich hedgerows and planted spinneys

Bluebell and orange-tip butterfly

The meadows provide evidence of bygone years, with ancient 'ridge and furrow' plough markings still evident. A traditional hay and grazing regime has enabled over 100 flowering plant species to flourish at this delightful reserve.

East Meadow gives rise to a mass of wild flowers in late spring and early summer with betony, yellow rattle and sneezewort. A community of great burnet dominates the grassland in summer, attracting many grassland butterflies. West Meadow, thanks to recent management, now hosts a multitude of grasses and ragged-robin, providing a home for numerous insects including a nationally scarce click beetle.

The diverse plant communities found at Deans Green offer its visitors an array of colour throughout the year, with bluebells and violets carpeting the spinneys. The fringing hedgerows containing mature tree and shrub species such as oak, ash, hazel and blackthorn, provide an abundance of colourful autumn fruits for over-wintering birds and other animals.

MANAGEMENT

Management of these meadows focuses on boundary fencing work, scrub removal, harvesting of a hay crop and cattle grazing.

GETTING THERE

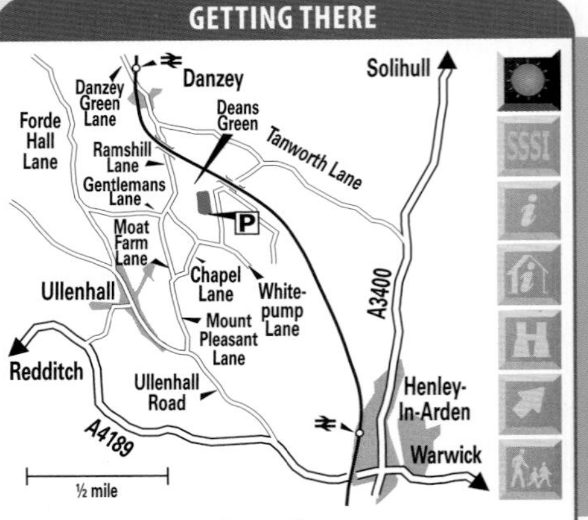

STATUS & FACILITIES

Deans Green
OS SHEET 151; SP 132 682

LOCATION 3 km north west of Henley-in-Arden, off Tanworth Lane towards Deans Green or off White Pump Lane.

P Car parking next to the gate or on lane.
Danzey + walk / cycle 1¼ miles.

GETTING AROUND

SIZE 4.5 ha (10.1 acres)
No defined paths, areas prone to waterlogging. Please keep to boundary.

Best time to visit

WINTER
BIRDS Woodpeckers, fieldfare, redwing

SPRING ✔
PLANTS Wood anemone, bluebell, wild service-tree, violets, cowslip

SUMMER ✔
PLANTS Betony, sneezewort, yellow rattle, great burnet, devil's-bit scabious
INSECTS Butterflies

AUTUMN ✔
PLANTS Hedgerow fruits and colour

Hornbeam catkins

Earlswood Moathouse

Created on pasture land within the National Trust's Earlswood Moathouse Estate, this shady reserve comprises planted woodland, ancient grassland and ponds

Formerly two open fields adjoining a small wood, the site was planted with some 3,000 broad-leaved trees and a dozen species of shrubs. Oak, ash, silver birch, hawthorn, blackthorn and dogwood formed the main bulk of these plantings with others such as wild cherry and guelder-rose making up the balance.

Today, the wood still reflects this mix with a number of additions including small-leaved lime, rowan and hazel. A magnificent line of hornbeam graces the eastern end and there are some fine yews.

Long-tailed tit, jay, nuthatch, treecreeper and the diminutive wren are regulars amongst the woodland, and obvious signs of badger and fox activity can be seen on the ground.

Although rather poor, the ground flora contains surprises like wood-sorrel, and autumn brings a range of fungi. One of the less shaded ponds supports a small community of bulrush, sedge and rush where a number of dragonflies display and great crested newt have established.

MANAGEMENT

The scrub and woodland on this site is managed by coppicing and by the creation of glades to allow light to reach the ground. The ponds and scrub around the ponds are cleared periodically and the paths maintained.

GETTING THERE

Stratford Canal
Earlswood
Earlswood Lakes
Birmingham
Umberslade Road
Malthouse Lane
Reservoir Hotel
M42
B4102
Bromsgrove
Tithe Barn Lane
M42
Warwick
M40
Wood End
B4101
1 mile

Earlswood Moathouse
OS SHEET 139; SP 116 736

LOCATION West of Dorridge, 1 km south of Earlswood, situated off the B4102 south of the junction with Umberslade Road.

P Car parking next to the Reservoir Hotel.
The Lakes + / ¾ mile.

GETTING AROUND

SIZE 3.9 ha (9.5 acres)
Flat, soft patches, kissing gate. Muddy at times.

STATUS & FACILITIES

SSSI

THE NATIONAL TRUST

Best time to visit

WINTER

SPRING ✔
PLANTS Trees and shrubs
AMPHIBIANS Great crested newt

SUMMER ✔
MAMMALS Badger signs

AUTUMN ✔
PLANTS Yew fruit, hornbeam

Reed bunting

Eathorpe Marsh

This little marsh with its shallow ponds adjoins the beautiful River Leam and supports an abundance of wetland wildlife

Towards the wetter centre of the marsh, greater pond-sedge dominates with some bulrush and common reed, where sedge warbler and reed bunting reside. Reed sweet-grass, wild angelica, bittersweet and marsh woundwort can also be found.

Shorter herbage round one pond supports marsh-marigold, cuckooflower, water mint and bog stitchwort, with water horsetail and lesser water-parsnip growing in the shallows.

The woodland next to the marsh has alder and various willows, plus oak, ash and elder, although the natural colonisation of the wood is restricted in order to maintain the open marsh.

Over 400 invertebrates have been recorded here with many beetles, flies, bees and spiders providing rich pickings for an array of birds.

MANAGEMENT

Management focuses on clearing ponds, removing invading willow from the marsh and pollarding large trees.

GETTING THERE

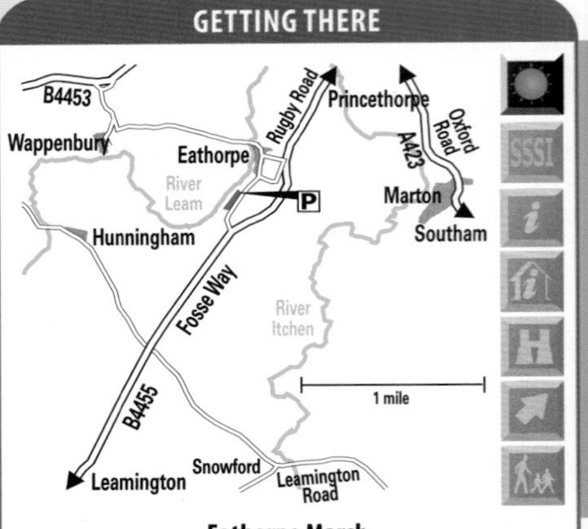

STATUS & FACILITIES

Eathorpe Marsh
OS SHEET 151; SP 389 687

LOCATION North-east of Leamington Spa. Turn off the B4455 Fosse Way to Eathorpe Village, park next to Severn Trent Water's pumping station. Visitors are requested to follow a circular path which runs around the perimeter of this reserve.

P Park in the Pumping Station next to the reserve.
Coventry + Leamington Spa stations + bus to Eathorpe + walk / cycle ¼ mile.

GETTING AROUND

SIZE 1.4 ha (3.5 acres)
Flat, soft patches, floods in winter, stiles
No dogs allowed on this reserve
Entry restricted – Members only

Severn Trent

Best time to visit

WINTER

SPRING ✔
PLANTS Willows, cuckooflower, marsh-marigold
BIRDS Sedge warbler, reed bunting

SUMMER ✔
PLANTS Marsh woundwort, lesser water-parsnip, water mint

AUTUMN ✔
BIRDS Snipe

Elmdon Manor

Once formal gardens of the Old Manor in the early 18th century, this secluded reserve comprises woodland, a meadow, ponds and a walled garden, reputedly the largest in England

Gatekeeper

Elmdon Manor fell into disrepair after the 2nd World War and was demolished, with its former grounds becoming public parkland until 1983. Following the neglect of the gardens in subsequent years, the Trust took over its management and set about improving the reserve.

Inside the garden's ivy-clothed walls, efforts have been made to re-establish the original fruit orchard where michaelmas daisy and rosebay willowherb provide a colourful display. Spring blossoms attract many bees, hoverflies and butterflies to this quintessential English orchard.

Outside the imposing walls, mature oak, elm and yew provide open woodland, attracting buzzard, sparrowhawk and jays. The re-establishment of a wildflower meadow gives rise to swathes of delightful flora, including cuckooflower, common knapweed and St John's-wort.

The old ponds add further diversity with bulrush, yellow iris and water mint giving shelter to much aquatic life.

MANAGEMENT

The grasslands within the walled garden and meadow are managed by cutting and sward removal in autumn. Additional maintenance work is carried out on the boundaries and footpaths.

GETTING THERE

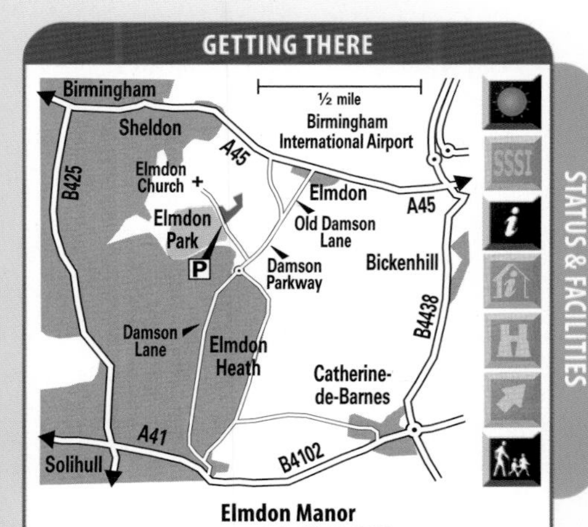

Elmdon Manor
OS SHEET 175; SU 616 795

LOCATION On the northern edge of Solihull, 0.5km south-west of Elmdon. Turn off Damson Parkway, near roundabout. Access is from the road leading to Elmdon Church.

P Park in lay-by opposite gate at entrance.
Solihull + bus to Wells Green + walk / cycle 1½ miles.

GETTING AROUND

SIZE 5 ha (12.5 acres)
Flat, soft patches, muddy in winter, clear footpaths

Best time to visit

WINTER

SPRING ✔
PLANTS Cuckooflower
AMPHIBIANS Common frog
BIRDS Birds of prey, little grebe

SUMMER ✔
PLANTS Sneezewort, common knapweed, St John's-wort

AUTUMN ✔
PLANTS Apple tree fruit, leaf colour

Amethyst deceiver

Glasshouse Spinney

Although this strip of mature woodland resembles a planted shelterbelt, its origins are significantly older and account for its pleasing diversity

The presence of flowers such as sweet woodruff, yellow archangel, lily-of-the-valley, wood melick, wood anemone and dog's mercury show that this land has been wooded since ancient times.

The site is home to a considerable population of English elm, with oak, sycamore, white poplar and common lime. Holly, blackthorn, hazel and dog-rose form the understorey whilst bramble and ivy carpet the ground.

Areas of sandy soil allow beech, silver birch and bracken to grow at the northern end of the reserve, providing fantastic displays of colour in the autumn.

A treasure trove of fungi including amethyst deceiver, false deathcap, turkeytail and dead man's fingers make for delightful viewing during this spectacular season.

MANAGEMENT

The Spinney is managed by coppicing, which enhances the ground flora and improves the age structure and diversity of the reserve.

GETTING THERE

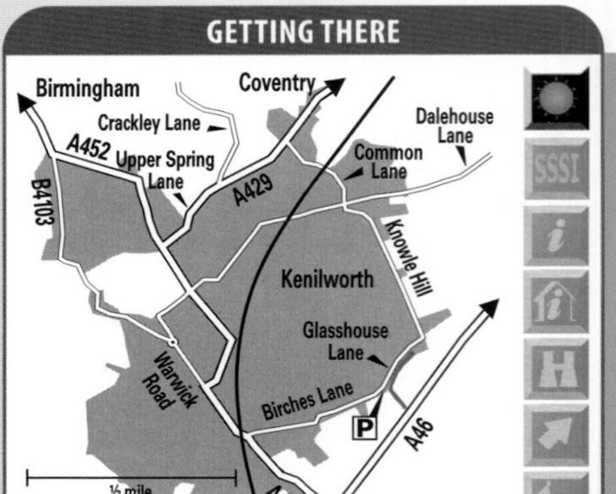

STATUS & FACILITIES

SSSI

Glasshouse Spinney
OS SHEET 140; SP 304 714

LOCATION On the south-east edge of Kenilworth, take Birches Lane off the A452, the reserve is on Glasshouse Lane before Knowle Hill.

P Park in lay-by on Glasshouse Lane at southern end of the wood.
Coventry + Leamington Spa stations + to Glasshouse Lane + / 1 mile.

GETTING AROUND

SIZE 1.5 ha (3.7 acres)
Flat, muddy in winter

Best time to visit

WINTER

SPRING ✔
PLANTS Sweet woodruff, wood anemone, lily-of-the-valley, yellow archangel

SUMMER ✔
PLANTS Laid beech hedge

AUTUMN ✔
FUNGI Amethyst deceiver, false deathcap, turkeytail, dead man's fingers
PLANTS Beech and bracken colour

Common spotted-orchid

Goldicote Cutting

Slashing through lower lias limestone, this deep disused railway cutting supports a multitude of limestone-loving flora

Goldicote Cutting's steep banks are densely clothed with scrub, enticing a good number of warblers, tits and finches during springtime.

Much of the cutting is very wet with areas of marshy ground prevalent at the eastern end of the reserve. A fine population of common spotted-orchid thrives here with impressive stands of giant horsetail. Willowherb, water figwort and common fleabane shade a stream where many scarce invertebrates, including an uncommon solider fly, relish the damp conditions.

Towards the western end of the cutting, limestone grassland produces a flourish of wild flowers, including bee orchid, hairy violet and yellow-wort. Many species of butterfly favour this site including the diminutive dingy and grizzled skippers. A colony of white-letter hairstreaks prosper on the elms. The reserve also offers one of the last remaining Warwickshire haunts to the inappropriately named common lizard, which can occasionally be seen sunbathing amongst the bricks.

MANAGEMENT

Management of the cutting in recent years has focused on maintaining paths and cutting the grassland.

GETTING THERE

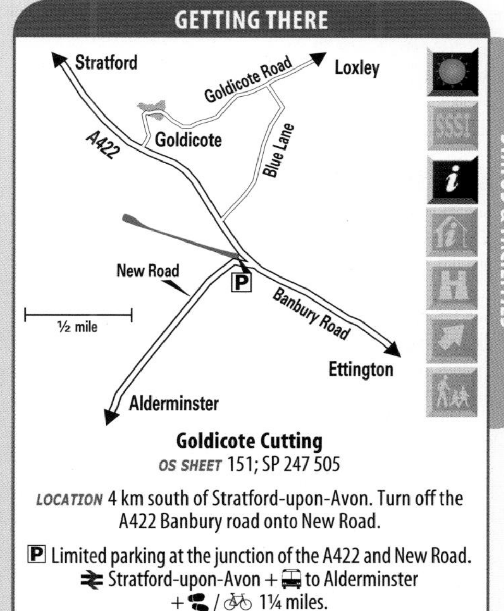

Goldicote Cutting
OS SHEET 151; SP 247 505

LOCATION 4 km south of Stratford-upon-Avon. Turn off the A422 Banbury road onto New Road.

P Limited parking at the junction of the A422 and New Road.
Stratford-upon-Avon + bus to Alderminster + walk / cycle 1¼ miles.

GETTING AROUND

SIZE 3 ha (7.4 acres)
Very steep slopes in parts, soft in patches
No dogs allowed on this reserve

Best time to visit

WINTER

SPRING ✔
PLANTS Hairy violet, cowslip
INSECTS Dingy and grizzled skipper butterflies
BIRDS Migrant warblers

SUMMER ✔
PLANTS Bee orchid, common spotted-orchid, grass vetchling
INSECTS White-letter hairstreak and common blue butterflies
REPTILES Common lizard

AUTUMN ✔
PLANTS Traveller's-joy fruit
BIRDS Woodland birds

Wild daffodil

Harvest Hill

This unimproved little meadow, edged with ancient hedgerows, is nestled to the north-west of Coventry and is especially noted for its wonderful display of wild daffodils during spring

Seasonally grazed by a small flock of Hebridian sheep in order to maintain the meadow and ensure the survival of the daffodil population, the reserve boasts a handful of woodland flowers such as bluebell and lesser celandine. Other typical meadow plants include pignut and cowslip, with coarser nettle, thistle and bracken attracting numerous insects.

At the bottom of the gentle slope a small pond was reinstated in the early 1980s and now supports bulrush, sedges and rushes with cuckooflower and meadowsweet. A number of aquatic creatures reside in its murky waters and newts have been recorded.

The laid hedgerow flanking Brick Lane supports a wealth of species including oak, ash, field maple, holly and blackthorn. Common dog-rose, ivy and bittersweet weave their way through, adding to the hedge's density and providing ideal nesting opportunities for many birds.

MANAGEMENT

Management largely involves maintaining the stock-proof fencing to provide a secure environment for the Hebridean sheep to graze in.

GETTING THERE

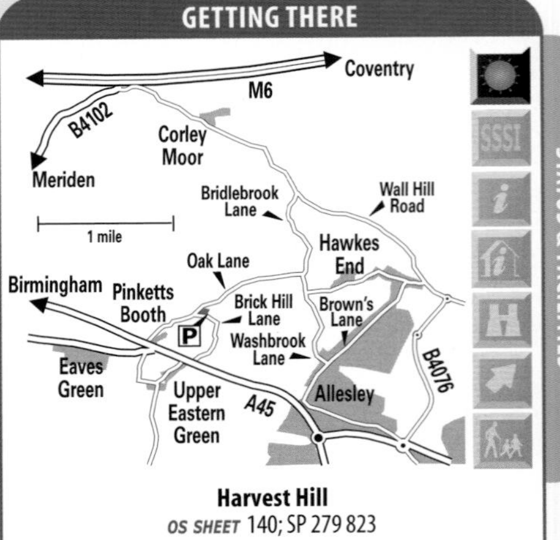

Harvest Hill
OS SHEET 140; SP 279 823

LOCATION 1 km to the north-west of Coventry, close to the village of Allesley.

P Limited verge parking, narrow lane.
Coventry bus to Allesley Village + / 2 miles.

GETTING AROUND

SIZE 0.6 ha (1.5 acres)
Relatively flat, stiles on access
No dogs allowed on this reserve

Best time to visit

WINTER

SPRING ✓
PLANTS Wild daffodil

PLANTS Ancient hedgerows
BIRDS Tits
MAMMALS Hebridean sheep

AUTUMN ✓
MAMMALS Hebridean sheep

Henley Sidings

Lying in a railway cutting, flanked by the Stratford-upon-Avon to Birmingham railway line, this former siding presents a slender wildlife gem for birds, butterflies and flowers

Marbled white butterfly

The reserve is noted for its limestone grassland, which has established on an area of lime-rich soils towards the northern end of the reserve.

Deposited on underlying Arden sandstone, this calcareous soil supports a galaxy of wild flowers including woolly thistle, fairy flax and lady's bedstraw. More neutral areas hold cowslip, wild carrot and oxeye daisy.

A high rabbit population maintains the sward and in some areas it is sufficiently sparse for a carpet of lichen to cover the ground. Yellow meadow ant hills provide an interesting feature and are worthy of note. Twenty species of butterfly have been recorded here, including marbled white and clouded yellow. Day-flying moths such as latticed heath and the narrow-bordered five-spot burnet provide further variety. Around 200 species of beetle have also been recorded.

This small reserve attracts feeding redwing and fieldfare during winter months, with the promise of warmer weather enticing chiffchaff, willow warbler and bullfinch in the spring.

MANAGEMENT

The limestone grassland at Henley Sidings is maintained by seasonal grass cutting, creation of glades and scrub clearance.

GETTING THERE

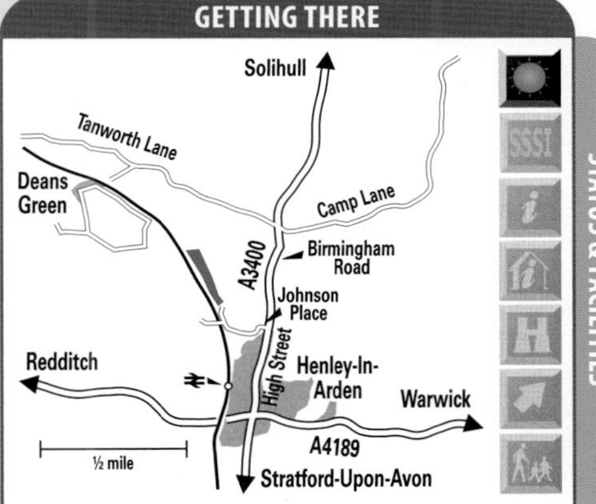

Henley Sidings
OS SHEET 151; SP 147 667

LOCATION 0.5 km north of Henley-in-Arden. Take the turning for Johnson Place off the A3400, High Street.

P Parking available in Henley in Arden, access via footpath off A3400 towards Henley Golf Club.
Henley-in-Arden + walk / cycle ½ mile.

GETTING AROUND

SIZE 1.4 ha (3.5 acres)
Prone to water-logging, soft in patches

Best time to visit

WINTER ✔
INSECTS Yellow meadow ant hills
BIRDS Redwing, fieldfare

SPRING ✔
PLANTS Cowslip
INSECTS Holly blue and orange-tip butterflies
BIRDS Migrant warblers

SUMMER ✔
PLANTS Agrimony, dwarf thistle, woolly thistle
INSECTS Marbled white and common blue butterflies, day-flying moths

AUTUMN ✔
PLANTS Lichens

Small copper butterfly

Knowle Hill

Surrounded by houses, this pleasant LNR forms an oasis of trees, shrubs and grassland offering a valuable refuge to much wildlife

Formerly unimproved pastureland, this urban reserve lies within the northern fringe of Kenilworth and now supports a diverse range of habitats.

Gorse, broom and bracken are relics of the site's former acidic heathland. Many wild flowers such as foxglove, harebell, sheep's sorrel, cuckooflower and bluebell favour this reserve.

There are many types of grasses including fescues and bents, Yorkshire-fog and smooth meadow-grass, which attract numerous insects.

Twenty-one species of butterfly are listed here, including purple hairstreak, marbled white and small copper.

MANAGEMENT

A wide variety of management tasks take place at Knowle Hill including; sycamore removal, Japanese knotweed control, scrub clearance, path maintenance and coppicing of woodland compartments.

GETTING THERE

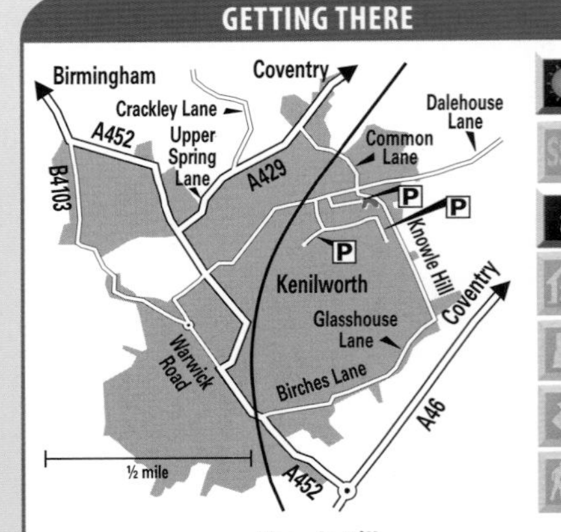

STATUS & FACILITIES

Knowle Hill

OS SHEET 140; SP 300 727

LOCATION On the north-east side of Kenilworth, situated off Knowle Hill close to the junction with Dalehouse Lane and Common Lane.

P Roadside parking on Greensward Close, Villiers Road, Rainsley Drive or on surrounding roads.
Coventry + bus to Knowle Hill.

GETTING AROUND

SIZE 4.1 ha (10.1 acres)
Steep slopes, informal paths

Best time to visit

WINTER ✔
PLANTS Gorse

SPRING ✔
PLANTS Broom, cuckooflower, bluebell

SUMMER ✔
PLANTS Harebell, meadow crane's-bill, foxglove
INSECTS Marbled white, small copper and purple hairstreak butterflies

AUTUMN ✔
BIRDS Sparrowhawk

White saddle

Lion Wood

This small, quiet oak wood sits on acidic, free-draining soils and supports a variety of interesting lime-hating plants

Located just outside the county border, the reserve is situated in the very north-east of neighbouring Worcestershire. Jointly owned by Warwickshire and Worcestershire Wildlife Trusts, the reserve is under the management of Worcestershire Wildlife Trust.

Lion Wood once formed part of the larger Brockhill Wood SSSI. Predominantly oak with frequent holly, birch, rowan and bilberry, the wood's acidic soils support plants such as wood sage, foxglove, heath bedstraw and wavy hair-grass.

Autumn provides a fantastic display of fungi with bonnets, amanitas, white saddle and aniseed funnel all thriving on the woodland floor.

MANAGEMENT

Managed by Worcestershire Wildlife Trust. Management aims to thin the woodland to promote growth of the bilberry and other acidic heathland ground flora and alder buckthorn.

GETTING THERE

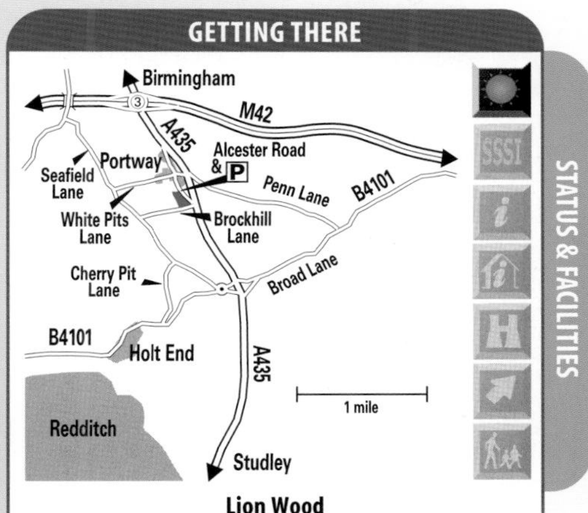

Lion Wood
OS SHEET 139; SP 085 717

LOCATION North of Redditch, 0.5 km south of Portway, on the junction of Brockhill Lane and Alcester Road off the main A435.

P Parking on Alcester Road – 'The Portway'.
Redditch + / 6 miles.

GETTING AROUND

SIZE 3.4 ha (8 acres)
Well defined informal paths, can become wet and muddy

WORCESTERSHIRE

Best time to visit

WINTER

SPRING

SUMMER ✔
PLANTS Bilberry, foxglove, wood sage

AUTUMN ✔
FUNGI Bonnets, amanitas, aniseed funnel, white saddle

Meadow brown butterfly

Parliament Piece

This charming reserve lies near the town of Kenilworth, its intriguing name relating to Henry III's parliament, rumoured to have met here in 1266

Designated an LNR, Parliament Piece offers a range of habitats with attractive open rough grassland, impressively tall trees, old hedgerows and a pond.

Managed as hay meadow, the grassland is dominated by coarse grasses, thistles and docks, providing ideal habitat for skipper and brown butterflies. Sometimes, hundreds of meadow brown can offer an impressive sight, dancing amongst the grass.

Great spotted woodpecker can often be seen or heard amongst the magnificent Turkey oaks, beech, field maple and Scots pine.

The ancient hedges, rich with hawthorn and wild cherry, are woven with dog-rose, ivy and traveller's-joy, suggesting an age of around 400 years, and provide wonderful nesting sites to a host of finches, tits and other songbirds.

The pond's shady waters, edged with ash and willow, provide a home to common frog and smooth newt which both spawn here in spring.

MANAGEMENT

Management of this grassland site includes cattle grazing and manual removal of scrub. In addition, the pond and surrounding scrub are cleared periodically.

GETTING THERE

Crackley Lane
Hollis Lane
Coventry
A452
Upper Spring Lane
A429
Coventry Road
B4103
High Street
New Street
B4103
Coventry
Kenilworth
A46
A452
1 mile
Leamington
Warwick

STATUS & FACILITIES
SSSI

Parliament Piece
OS SHEET 140; SP 288 729

LOCATION On the northern edge of Kenilworth, off Upper Spring Lane.

P Parking at site entrance (stile) off Upper Spring Lane.
Coventry + bus to Kenilworth, stops at watertower close to reserve .

GETTING AROUND

SIZE 6.1 ha (15.1 acres)
Flat, informal paths, muddy in winter.
Access via stiles/kissing gates

Best time to visit

WINTER

SPRING ✔

AMPHIBIANS Common frog, smooth newt
BIRDS Finches and tits
MAMMALS Field vole

SUMMER ✔

PLANTS Turkey oak, dog-rose, traveller's-joy
INSECTS Meadow brown butterfly

AUTUMN

Priory Fields

A true wildlife gem surrounded by housing, this reserve forms part of a valuable 'green corridor' on the border of Solihull and Birmingham

Blackberries

Comprising four fields, this peaceful oasis is bisected by Mill Stream, which feeds the large mill pool sitting adjacent to the reserve.

Predominantly moss and swampland in 972AD, the site gave rise to heath and pasture by 1495, and eventually became Yardley Wood Common until 1847.

Changing little since, the site still offers remnants of heathland and acidic grassland, now rare habitats in Warwickshire. Heather, broom, dwarf gorse and heath rush occupy one of the four fields, with carnation sedge, marsh-marigold and lesser spearwort present along the stream's damp margins.

Hawthorn and blackthorn produce valuable scrub, attracting over 60 species of birds throughout the year; with oaks, silver birch, rowan and exotic red oak adding height.

Hedges are dense with bramble, which produce juicy clusters of autumn blackberries for a host of birds and small mammals, and pies!

MANAGEMENT

Management is mainly focused around cutting the meadow and turf stripping to try and encourage the heather to regenerate.

GETTING THERE

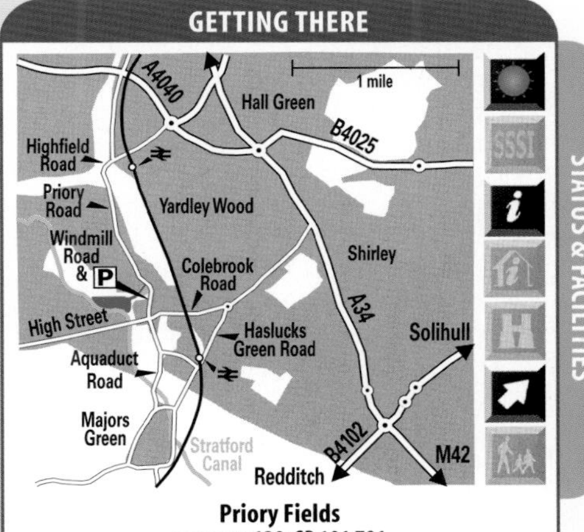

Priory Fields

OS SHEET 139; SP 101 791

LOCATION On the boundary between Birmingham and Solihull, the reserve is situated on Priory Road close to the junction with High Street.

P Parking on verge on Priory Road.

Shirley + walk / cycle 1 mile.

GETTING AROUND

SIZE 5.4 ha (13 acres)

Flat, informal paths, muddy in winter

Birmingham City Council

Best time to visit

WINTER

SPRING ✔
PLANTS Marsh-marigold

SUMMER ✔
PLANTS Heather, dwarf gorse, lesser spearwort

AUTUMN ✔
PLANTS Blackberries

Kingfisher

River Arrow

Near the centre of historic Alcester, this idyllic LNR consists of beautiful stretches of river bank, flower-rich grassland, delightful woodland and a deep pool

The rushing river, with chub and pike, constantly erodes its banks, leaving pebbly shores for hemlock, feeding grey wagtails and several scarce county beetles. The banks are irregularly edged with willows, alder, oak and hawthorn providing ideal perches for kingfishers. In summer purple-loosestrife, great willowherb and fool's water-cress line the pool where mallard and moorhen hatch their broods. Water boatmen and whirligig beetles swirl on the pool's surface, while dragonflies and damselflies dart busily by.

The meadows have few wild flowers but a variety of grasses. Flowers such as bird's-foot-trefoil, burnet-saxifrage and yarrow can be found in the northern meadow. The woodland strip comprises ash, oak, alder and willow with towering Scots pine, hazel and blackthorn, and is home to both great spotted and green woodpecker.

Outside the reserve stands the privately owned Ragley Mill, first mentioned in 1241. Abbey Field, with its remains of a Benedictine abbey dated 1140, was added to the LNR in 2002, bringing further beauty to this attractive site.

MANAGEMENT

Management involves cutting back invading scrub and maintaining the pathways. Grassland management is carried out by grazing sheep.

GETTING THERE

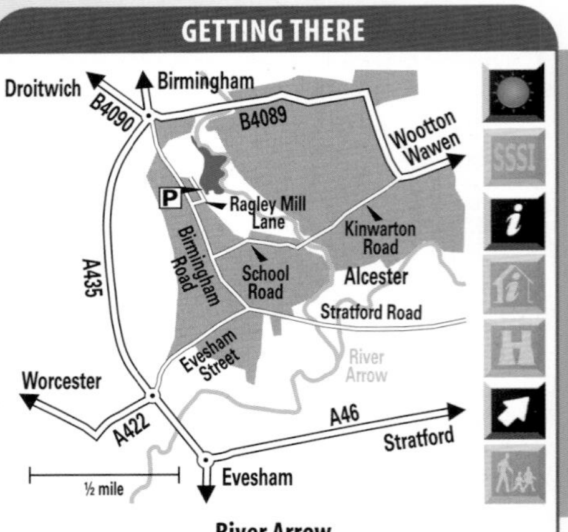

River Arrow

OS SHEET 150; SO 086 581

LOCATION Near the centre of Alcester. Take Ragley Mill Lane off Birmingham Road, parking on Ragley Mill Lane.

P Parking on Ragley Mill Lane.

Stratford-upon-Avon + bus to Alcester + walk / cycle ¼ mile.

GETTING AROUND

SIZE 3 ha (7.4 acres)

Relatively flat, soft patches, access via kissing gate. Disabled access to pond

Best time to visit

WINTER

SPRING ✔

PLANTS Willows

BIRDS Kingfisher, moorhen, grey wagtail, woodpeckers

SUMMER ✔

PLANTS Small teasel, purple-loosestrife

INSECTS Dragonflies and damselflies

REPTILES Grass snake

AUTUMN

Stoke Floods

A mosaic of wetland, tall herb, rough grassland and scrub, this LNR occupies the floodplain of the River Sowe forming a vital part of the Sowe Valley Green Corridor

Tufted duck

The reserve's prominent feature is the large pool, created through mining subsidence, that now attracts over 90 species of birds, many of which breed here including grebes, warblers and water rail. The lake is vital for overwintering birds and is a regular haunt for tufted duck, shoveler and snipe.

The pool's gently sloping edges permit stands of willow, reed, bulrush and reed canary-grass, which provide excellent cover. Purple-loosestrife and yellow iris provide contrasting summer colour.

To the east and west the swamp grades from marsh into rough grassland and tall herb. Meadowsweet, great willowherb and meadow crane's-bill flourish. The northern woodland is dominated by sycamore, horse-chestnut and is valuable for songbirds such as tits and finches.

Several nationally notable invertebrates have been recorded here, with surveys identifying 242 species of beetle alone.

MANAGEMENT

The management largely involves maintaining the pathways which bisect the wetland scrub area around the back of the lake.

GETTING THERE

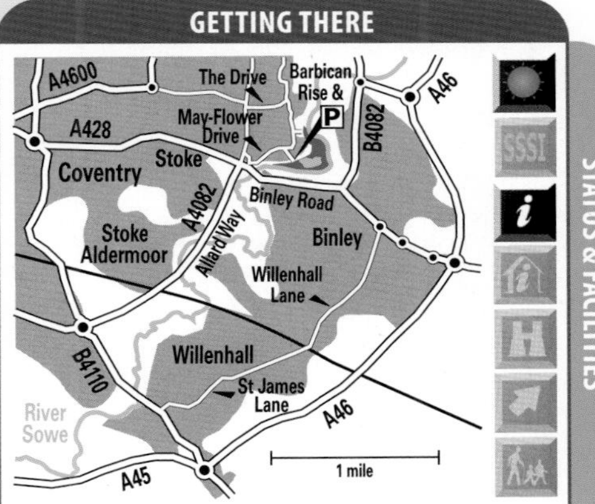

STATUS & FACILITIES

Stoke Floods

OS SHEET 140; SP 370 785

LOCATION On the east side of Coventry, turn off the A428 opposite the junction with Allard Way. At the mini roundabout take the third exit. Turn first right onto Mayflower Drive, Barbican Rise is the 4th turning on right.

P Limited parking at the end of Barbican Rise.
Coventry + bus to Stoke + walk / cycle ¼ mile.

GETTING AROUND

SIZE 7.7 ha (19 acres)
Relatively flat, soft patches, parts of the site flood in winter

Best time to visit

WINTER ✔

BIRDS Tufted duck, shoveler, snipe

SPRING ✔

PLANTS Yellow iris
BIRDS Migrant warblers, grebes, kingfisher

SUMMER ✔

PLANTS Meadow crane's-bill, purple-loosestrife. nodding bur-marigold
BIRDS Water rail

AUTUMN

Temple Balsall

Now shady damp woodland, this reserve was formerly an exotic water garden of the Springfield Estate

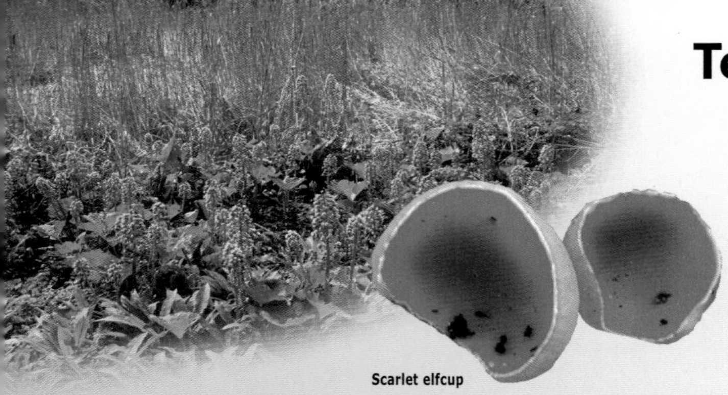

Scarlet elfcup

Diverse in wildlife, this pleasant wet woodland is bisected by Cuttle Brook as it makes its way to join the River Blythe.

The marshy ground here results from the past existence of an artificial lake that occupied this site before its destruction during the late 1940s. Common reed and sedges occupy the wetter areas, and there is also a stand of butterbur which produces impressive umbrella-sized leaves in summer.

Although many plants such as bamboo and rhododendron are introductions, the reserve is rich in native flowers and gives a fine show of snowdrops and ramsons in the spring. Scarcer species include large bittercress and opposite-leaved golden-saxifrage.

Alder and willow thrive on the wet soils. The former produces seeds which provide rich pickings for birds such as siskin. The reserve has also produced excellent lists of insects and fungi, with scarlet elfcup bringing startling colour to these unfrequented woods in the winter.

MANAGEMENT

Management on this site focuses on maintaining open water in the pond and preventing succession to woodland in this area.

GETTING THERE

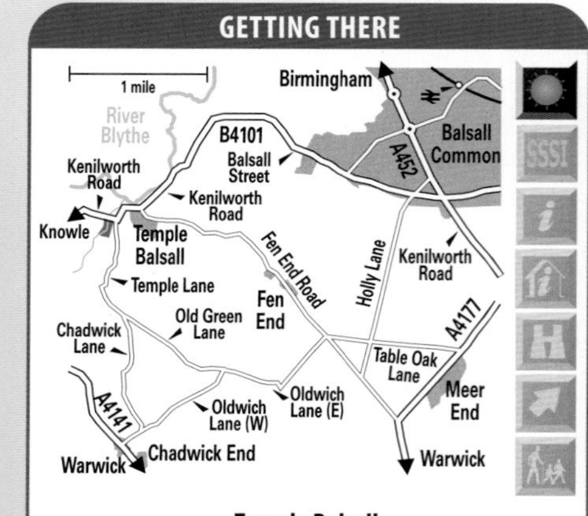

STATUS & FACILITIES

SSSI

Temple Balsall
OS SHEET 139; SP 203 760

LOCATION 2.5 km west of Balsall Common, situated in the village of Temple Balsall. Reserve can be found on the junction of Temple Lane and the B4101 Kenilworth Road.

P Parking available in Temple Balsall.
Dorridge or Berkswell. No197 from Knowle or Balsall Common to Temple Balsall + / ¼ mile.

GETTING AROUND

SIZE 2.7 ha (6.6 acres)
Flat, paths can get muddy, kissing gates

Birmingham City Council

Best time to visit

WINTER ✔
FUNGI Scarlet elfcup
PLANTS Snowdrop

SPRING ✔
PLANTS Ramsons, butterbur, opposite-leaved golden-saxifrage, large bittercress
MAMMALS Badger activity

SUMMER ✔
PLANTS Giant bellflower, yellow iris, water-plantain, butterbur leaves

AUTUMN ✔
BIRDS Siskin

Alder catkins

Whitnash Brook

This small LNR is a wildlife gem of damp, rough grassland, pools, hedgerows and woodland

This valuable wildlife corridor was once dominated by rough, species-poor grassland and scrub until recent enhancement through the creation of a number of pools. These already support a significant variety of wetland plants such as brooklime and lesser water-parsnip, and provide an excellent place to watch dragonflies in the summer.

The shaded stream supports mature alder and willow, some of which have been pollarded. Fallen trees provide a wealth of niches for small mammals and invertebrates.

Oak and ash are the main trees with remnant elm, crab apple, hawthorn and elder. Sycamore appears to the north with introduced Norway maple, beech, horse-chestnut and some large hybrid black-poplars also present.

The hedgerows host guelder-rose, hazel, dogwood and hornbeam, with ivy and dog-rose frequent. Many bird species flourish here with tits and finches seeking cover within the hedgerows and great spotted woodpecker nesting in the trees.

MANAGEMENT

Management focuses on removing scrub and young trees to prevent succession on grassland and open areas.

GETTING THERE

Coventry
1 mile
A445
A452
Leamington Spa
River Leam
B4099
High Street
A425
Radford Road
B4087
Grand Union Canal
Sydenham Drive
Otters Rest & P
Southam
Prospect Road
St Helens Road
Radford Semele
Whitnash
Chesterton Drive

STATUS & FACILITIES

SSSI

Whitnash Brook

OS SHEET 151; SP 334 642

LOCATION South-east of Leamington Spa. Turn off the A425 onto Sydenham Drive. At the end of road take first left at the mini roundabout onto Chesterton Drive, follow the road around into Otters Rest.

P Parking available in Otters Rest, off Chesterton Drive.
Leamington Spa + bus to Sydenham + walk / cycle ¼ mile.

GETTING AROUND

SIZE 4.9 ha (9.8 acres)

Kissing gate at Otters Rest, stone covered path good all year round.

Best time to visit

WINTER ✔
BIRDS Tits and finches

SPRING ✔
PLANTS Hybrid black-poplar, hawthorn and blackthorn blossom

SUMMER ✔
PLANTS Lesser water-parsnip, brooklime
INSECTS Dragonflies

AUTUMN ✔
PLANTS Leaf colour

Mute swan

Wyken Slough

Wyken Slough owes its original formation to mining subsidence in the early 20th century

This well-visited reserve forms the northern end of the Sowe Valley Green Corridor, which links the reserve to both Stoke Floods and Stonebridge Meadow reserves. Regardless of its urban siting, Wyken Slough remains one of the largest areas of grassland in Coventry. With its combination of grassland and surprisingly good wetland habitat, the site is rich in botanical interest and represents an important 'green lung' within the city.

Great willowherb, wild angelica and gypsywort grace the water's edge and the large shallow pool, which proves the largest area of water in Coventry, provides a breeding ground for a host of dragonfly and damselfly species, such as the brown and migrant hawkers.

The reserve welcomes a rich and varied bird life to the pool. A sizeable flock of mute swans and other waterfowl reside here with the marsh offering welcome coverage to reed bunting, meadow pipit and even the occasional jack snipe.

MANAGEMENT

Management is focused on the reedbed. Blocks are cut and removed each year by volunteers to improve the habitat for wetland birds.

GETTING THERE

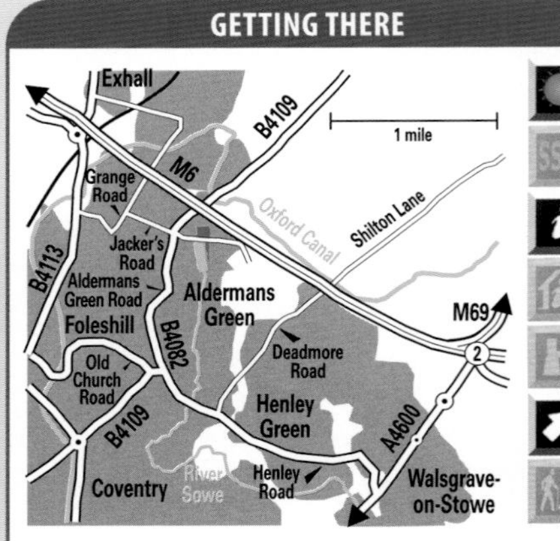

STATUS & FACILITIES

Wyken Slough
OS SHEET 140; SP 362 835

LOCATION On the northern edge of Coventry, access can be gained off the B4082, Aldermans Green Road.

P Park in the public car park on Alderman's Green Road (B4109).
Coventry + bus to Alderman's Green + walk / cycle ¼ mile.

GETTING AROUND

SIZE 1.2 ha (3 acres)
Relatively flat, wheelchair access to part of the site

Best time to visit

SUMMER ✔
PLANTS Devil's-bit scabious, gypsywort, great willowherb
INSECTS Brown hawker and migrant hawker dragonflies
BIRDS Ducks, mute swan, sedge warbler, reed bunting

WINTER ✔
BIRDS Redwing, fieldfare

SPRING

AUTUMN

Other nature reserves managed by Warwickshire Wildlife Trust

Cox's Island

LOCATION Cox's Island is located between Clopton Bridge and Tramway Bridge in the centre of Stratford-upon-Avon at Grid Ref SP 205 548

This small island forms an integral part of the riverside scene in Stratford-upon-Avon and was established as a memorial to Philip Handy. It lies in the River Avon and is an important refuge for mute swans. The island is predominantly wooded with mature hazel stools, suggesting an age of around 300 years. There is no public access to the site, although it can be viewed from the nearby bridge.

Hunningham Meadow LNR

LOCATION Hunningham, entrance at Grid Ref SP 373 680, parking along the north boundary

This little reserve comprises a 1.2 ha (3 acre) area of grassland which is managed as a hay meadow, and is edged by mature hedgerows.

Mill Close Meadow

LOCATION South of the B4101 Knowle to Temple Balsall road at Grid Ref SP 201 755

This 0.8 ha (2 acre) privately owned, meadow reserve was created with the turf from Shelley Green Hay Meadow, which was sadly destroyed for development in 1987, and lies 0.5 km south-west of Temple Balsall.

Oakwood and Blacklow Spinneys

LOCATION The spinneys lie between Blacklow Road and Oakwood Grove in the north of Warwick at Grid Ref SP 293 663

Once surrounded by open countryside, this small, 1.5 ha (4 acre) woodland LNR is now surrounded by urban development. The woodland is very diverse, providing welcome refuge to much wildlife in an otherwise urban landscape. Managed by an active volunteer group, the Friends of Oakwood and Blacklow Spinney campaigned to protect the site from development, ensuring the future survival of this pleasant little reserve.

Tysoe Island

LOCATION On the right hand side of the Shipston Road heading out of Upper Tysoe at Grid Ref SP 333 435

This deceptively named little reserve consist a small area of meadow and woodland which is bisected by a small stream. The remnant ancient grassland contains some pleasing flowers and meadow plants and the plantation woodland contains mixed native trees and shrubs.

Windmill Spinney

LOCATION Windmill Spinney is on Edyvean Close, off Bawnmore Road in the south of Rugby at Grid Ref SP 493 728

Formally part of a large garden this 0.6 ha (1.5 acre) reserve is now dominated by an interesting mix of trees and shrubs, which provide a valuable habitat for many birds.

Visitor Centres

Brandon Marsh Nature Centre

Just 15 minutes from Coventry City Centre, Brandon Marsh Nature Centre includes a SSSI Nature Reserve – a peaceful haven for a wide variety of wildlife – plus a Visitor Centre for events and information. Enjoy the following facilities all year round:

- 92 ha (228 acres) nature reserve
- 7 bird hides
- 10 pools
- Nature trails
- Sensory garden
- Interactive display area
- Conference facility
- Tea room
- Gift shop
- Excellent wheelchair access (mobility scooter available if pre-booked)

Parkridge Centre

Set in the middle of Brueton Park, on the edge of Solihull Town Centre, Parkridge Centre offers a tranquil setting for environmental education, plus a wide variety of nature conservation events and activities throughout the year. Its excellent facilities include:

- 2 ha (5 acre) nature park
- Education centre
- Interactive displays
- Tea room
- Wildlife gift shop

Family fun page
Water Wings

In **spring**, ducks and other wetland birds are very busy finding mates and building nests. Soon they will lay eggs from which little ducklings or chicks will eventually hatch. Some ducks and wetland birds even fly to Britain from other countries to breed.

See how many of these ducks and wetland birds you can spot swimming or paddling around in lakes and ponds.

When you have spotted them don't forget to write down when and where you saw them. Some are easy and some are a bit harder and you may need to visit a few nature reserves to find them.

Mallard

Where to look: In parks, on canals, rivers and ponds – anywhere where there's water! You can find them near the Parkridge Centre in Brueton Park or on all these nature reserves: Brandon Marsh, Whitacre Heath, Wyken Slough, Newbold Quarry and Welches Meadow.

Clue: The male *drakes* have green heads and the female *ducks* have a blue flash amongst their brown feathers.

When seen:

Where seen:

Great crested grebe

Where to look: Lakes and rivers with reeds where they can hide. You can find them on these nature reserves: Brandon Marsh, Pooley Fields, Whitacre Heath and Stoke Floods.

Clue: Long, slender neck and a 'punky' crest as summer approaches. In winter it has a shorter black cap on its head.

When seen:

Where seen:

Pochard

Where to look: They like to breed on marshy lakes. You can find them on these nature reserves: Brandon Marsh, Whitacre Heath and Newbold Quarry

Clue: The male *drakes* have reddish brown heads and bright red eyes.

When seen:

Where seen:

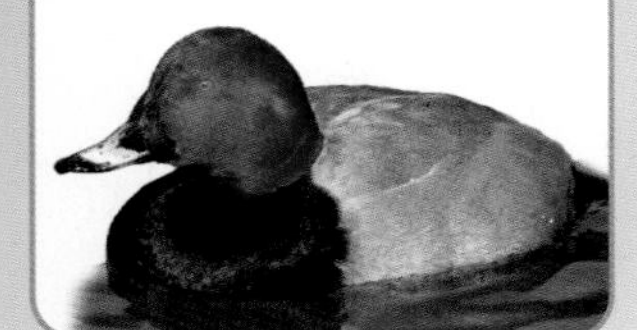

Tufted duck

Where to look: Lakes , park lakes, reservoirs and gravel pits. You can find them on these nature reserves: Newbold Quarry, Stoke Floods, Whitacre Heath, Swift Valley and Leam Valley.

Clue: They have bright yellow eyes and a funny hairstyle!

When seen:

Where seen:

Moorhen

Where to look: Parks, ponds and lakes. You can find them near the Parkridge Centre in Brueton Park or on all these nature reserves: Brandon Marsh, Pooley Fields, Swift Valley and River Arrow.

Clue: When they swim they nod their heads. The top of their beaks are bright red.

When seen:

Where seen:

Family fun page
We're going on a butterfly hunt

In **summer**, butterflies are very busy flying from flower to flower in search of pollen to eat. Lots of butterflies are very fussy eaters and only like to eat pollen from certain flowers!

Some butterflies like flowers that live in woods and some like flowers that grow in meadows or near water. If you find where the flowers live, you can try and spot the butterflies fluttering around nearby.

When you see each kind of butterfly, write down where and when you saw it below:

White admiral

Look for white admiral butterflies near these flowers: Honeysuckle and bramble flowers

You might find this butterfly on these nature reserves: Wappenbury and Old Nun Wood and Ryton Wood.

Clue: Look out for the big white bands on its black wings!

When seen:

Where seen:

Peacock

Look for peacock butterflies near these plants: nettles, teasel and thistles

You might find this butterfly on these nature reserves: Welcombe Hills, Ryton Wood and Brandon Marsh.

Clue: Look for big colourful eyes on their wings

When seen:

Where seen:

Brimstone

Look for brimstone butterflies near these plants: Buckthorn

You might find this butterfly on these nature reserves: Grove Hill, Hampton Wood and Meadow and Harbury Spoilbank

Clue: Brimstones can often be seen along hedgerows or on scrub land and woody areas. The males are bright yellow, the females light yellow.

When seen:

Where seen:

Holly blue

Look for holly blue butterflies near these plants: holly, ivy, spindle, gorse and bramble

You might find this butterfly on these nature reserves: Harbury Spoilbank, Stockton Cutting and Henley Sidings.

Clue: Often seen flying high around bushes and trees.

When seen:

Where seen:

Purple hairstreak

Look for purpule hairstreak butterflies near these trees: all oak species

You might find this butterfly on these nature reserves: Wappenbury Wood, Lion Wood and Rough Hill Wood.

Clue: Look for groups of oak trees, they might have a favourite tree which they hang around.

When seen:

Where seen:

Family fun page
If you go down to the woods today....

In **autumn**, lots of trees lose their leaves as the weather gets colder. Trees that lose their leaves are called 'deciduous' trees.

Look on the floor for the fallen leaves. The shape and size of the leaf will tell you what type of tree the leaf came from.

See if you can find the leaves from these trees next time you go for a walk. Write down where and when you saw them below:

Silver birch

Where to look: Birch trees can be seen on these nature reserves: Clowes Wood and New Fallings Coppice, Kenilworth Common and Crackley Wood.

Clue: After rain, birches exude a fragrant odour.

When seen:

Where seen:

Alder

Where to look: Marshes, riversides, lake sides and wet woodlands. You might find it on these nature reserves: Rough Hill Wood and Stockton Cutting.

Clue: The leaves do not change colour before they fall off in autumn.

When seen:

Where seen:

Oak

Where to look: Deciduous woodland. Oak trees can be seen on these nature reserves: Ryton Wood, Crackley Wood and Lion Wood.

Clue: If you see acorns on the ground you are getting very warm. Acorns come from oak trees too!

When seen:

Where seen:

Crab apple

Where to look: In oak woodlands, at the edges of woodland, on scrub or in hedgerows. Crab apple can be found on the following nature reserves: Wappenbury Wood and Old Nun Wood and Hampton Wood and Meadow.

Clue: Look out for the little yellow apples, sometimes tinged with red. Beware eating them though – they taste really sour!

When seen:

Where seen:

Ash

Where to look: Woodlands and on the banks of rivers and streams. Ash trees can be found on these nature reserves: Wappenbury and Old Nun Wood, Hampton Wood and Meadow and Earlswood Moathouse.

Clue: Look out for the ash keys – bunches of seeds encased in slightly twisted wings.

When seen:

Where seen:

Family fun page
Watch the birdie

Lots of birds fly away for the **winter** because they don't like the cold! However, some tough little birds stick around. They are much easier to see in winter because lots of the trees are bare so there are less leaves for them to hide behind!

See how many of these birds you can find. Some are easy and some are harder. Don't forget to write down when and where you saw them!

Robin

Where to look: Woods, gardens, parks and hedgerows. You can find them on these nature reserves: Wappenbury Wood and Old Nun Wood, Ryton Wood and Brandon Marsh.

Clue: You can't miss his reddy orange breast.

When seen:

Where seen:

Blue tit

Where to look: Deciduous and mixed woodland, parks and gardens. You can find them on these nature reserves: Kenilworth Common, Parliament Piece and Lion Wood.

Clue: Bright yellow tummy and a bright blue cap.

When seen:

Where seen:

Song thrush

Where to look: Woodland, parks, hedges and gardens. You can find them on these nature reserves: Welcombe Hills, Harvest Hill and Ryton Wood.

Clue: This bird has a really spotty chest but a beautiful trilling song.

When seen:

Where seen:

Great spotted woodpecker

Where to look: Deciduous woodland. You can find them on these nature reserves: Kenilworth Common, Welcombe Hills and Clowes Wood and New Fallings Coppice.

Clue: You will hear it before you see it. Listen for a loud hammering noise high in the trees as it drills the bark for insects to eat.

When seen:

Where seen:

Kingfisher

Where to look: By streams and rivers. You can find them on these nature reserves: Brandon Marsh, River Leam and River Arrow.

Clue: Look for their distinctive bright blue plumage and long beaks. They may be seen sitting on perches ready to go fishing.

When seen:

Where seen:

Volunteering

As a charity, volunteering remains vital to every aspect of the work of Warwickshire Wildlife Trust. We are dependent on volunteers to enable us to work to protect our environment for future generations. Volunteers bring new ideas and unique skills and knowledge to the Trust and their commitment and belief in our work strengthens us as an organisation. Without volunteers we would not be able to do half as much.

We aim to encourage people from all walks of life, with a variety of life experiences, to come along and get involved in our work. Certain roles require specific skills or experience but most allow you to learn as you go along, after receiving appropriate on-the-job training and guidance from a staff member or experienced volunteer. You decide how much time you are able to offer to the Trust – some people are able to volunteer every week whereas some are only available once a month or once a year – but however much time you can give will be greatly appreciated by all at the Trust.

There are a variety of different ways in which you can help and we will be extremely grateful for your support, whichever way you choose to give it. You could be helping us to manage our nature reserves by taking part in practical conservation work parties, surveying your local reserve or by acting as the "eyes and ears" of Warwickshire Wildlife Trust on the ground as a reserve warden. Alternatively, you could be helping our education team to deliver their programme of activities, aimed at providing children with a fun but educational way to learn about wildlife. You could also take part in local community projects, help run our visitor centres or come along and lend a helping hand in the offices. Every contribution is vital to our work so if you would like more information about the opportunities available please get in touch.

Volunteer Development Officer
Warwickshire Wildlife Trust
Brandon Marsh Nature Centre
Brandon Lane
Coventry
CV3 3 GW
Tel: 024 7630 2912
Email: volunteer@wkwt.org.uk

Glossary

AONB: Area of Outstanding Natural Beauty
Acid grassland : grassland on acid soils with a pH of below 7.0.
Aftermath grazing: grazing after taking a crop of hay or silage
Alluvial soil: soils developed within a river's flood plain
Artificial habitat: habitat created by humans
Biodiversity: the variety of plant and animal life
Calcareous grassland: grassland that has developed over chalk or limestone based soils
Calcareous soil: alkaline soil with a pH of above 7.0
Carr: wet woodland often dominated by willow and sallow
Clear-felling: removal of large areas of trees
Coppice: to cut trees or scrub to encourage regeneration from the stumps
Diversity: variety
Flood meadow: area of grassland within a river's flood plain
Flood plain: the low area of a valley floor, adjacent to a river which is periodically flooded
Glades: clear areas of ground found in woodlands, often grassy due to increased light
Hedge-laying: traditional hedgerow management to create a stock-proof barrier
Landscape-scale conservation: conserving areas for wildlife on a landscape scale
LBAP: Local Biodiversity Action Plan
LNR: Local Nature Reserve
Meadow: grassland cut for hay or silage
Neutral pasture/meadow: grassland developed over soils that are neither acidic nor alkaline
Non-native: introduced species from other regions or countries
Pasture: permanent grassland that is regularly grazed by livestock
Pollard/ing: method of managing trees by cutting the stem at head height or higher and letting it sprout.
Rides: wide grassy tracks created through woodland
Ridge and furrow: medieval plough markings
Saplings: young trees
Scallop/ing: coppiced areas adjacent to rides
Scarp slope: steep sided slope of a hill
Scrub: collective term for young trees and shrubs
Spoilheap: soil and/or vegetation removed during dredging
SSSI: Site of Special Scientific Interest – a conservation designation awarded to a site for its biological or geological interest
Standard: a woodland or hedgerow tree having a single stem and left to grow so as to be suitable for timber
Stool: the stump of a tree or shrub cut back to ground level
Sward: an area of grass or other low vegetation
Wet flush: an area of soil in which nutrients accumulate due to water inflow
Wet woodland: woodland that has developed over areas of damp ground or marshland
Wetland: marshland or area where the soil near the surface is saturated or covered with water

Species index

INSECTS

CRUSTACEANS

FISHES

AMPHIBIANS

REPTILES

BIRDS

MAMMALS

Nature reserves index

Sources of photographs

© E. Asbery
Volunteers (117 top)

© J. Asher
Brimstone (58,115), common blue (71), holly blue (115), orange-tip (88), peacock (115), purple hairstreak (115), silver birch (114), white admiral (115)

© D. Bright
Great crested grebe (113), reed bunting (27,96), woodcock (18)

© S. Cheshire
Grass snake (47)

© P. Creed
Alder (114), alder catkins (109), amethyst deceiver (98), ash (114), autumn gentian (58), betony (74), blackberry (105), blackthorn (52), bluebell (legacy page), blue fleabane (46), broad-leaved helleborine (76), bulbous buttercup (1), bulrush (41), carline thistle (72), celery-leaved buttercup (37), common puffball (79), common spotted-orchid (48,99), cowslip (70), crab apple (43,114), cuckooflower (66), devil's-bit scabious (53), dog-rose (59), dropwort (75), early forgetmenot (63), false saffron milkcap (38), fly agaric (64), fragrant agrimony (78), gatekeeper (97), gorse (50), grass vetchling (50), green-winged orchid (3,22), guelder-rose (93), hawthorn (5), hazel (60), hemlock water-dropwort (25), hornbeam (95), little grebe (46), marbled white (80,101), marsh-marigold (84), meadow brown (104), meadow foxtail (70), meadow thistle (52), oak (114), parasitic bolete (28), ragged-robin (68), scarlet elfcup (108), shaggy parasol (60), small copper (102), spurge-laurel (82), tawny grisette (56), water mint (92), white saddle (103), wild daffodil (100), wood anemone (19,77), wood white (5, legacy page), woolly thistle (90), yellow archangel (42), yellow iris (6,89), yellow pimpernel (28), yellow water-lily (35)

© Environment Agency
White-clawed crayfish (72)

© N. Jarvis
Bee orchid (73), purple hairstreak (45)

© E. Jones
Brandon Marsh Visitor Centre (112)

© D. Kjaer
Blue tit (116), common frog (26), jay (21), lesser spotted woodpecker (76), linnet (24), mallard (113), moorhen (36,113), muntjac (28), roe deer (78), skylark (69), teal (14,88)

© M. Lane
Skylark (74)

© S. Leszczynska
Volunteers (117 bottom)

© C. Marsay
Noctule bat (84), reserve picture (45), tawny owl (56)

© J. Milne
Kingfisher (46,106,116), siskin (64)

© D. Payne
Reserve picture (20)

© M. Read
Cuckoo fledgling (31), pochard (113)

© J. Roberts
Adder's-tongue fern (32), autumn gentian (62), banded demoiselle (88), beefsteak fungus (86), bilberry (18), bracken (58), broad-bodied chaser (39), broom (64), brown hawker (72), buckthorn (82), chimney-sweeper moth (32), cinnabar oysterling (42), comma (90), common bird's-foot-trefoil (32), common blue (22), common frog (34), common spotted-orchid (54), cowslip (22), dog-rose (62), emperor dragonfly (54), fly agaric (24), four-spotted chaser (14), fritillary (66), glow-worm (64), grass snake (66), great burnet (52), greater butterfly-orchid (82), great willowherb (86), green hairstreak (62), green tiger beetle (82), grizzled skipper (58), hairy dragonfly (24), harebell (84), hart's-tongue (86), herb-Paris (78), highland cattle (37), holly (76), holly blue (82), honeysuckle (42), horn-of-plenty (76), horse mushroom (84), jellybabies (14), lily-of-the-valley (18), man orchid (38), marbled white (50), meadow waxcap (32), midland hawthorn (74), opposite-leaved golden-saxifrage (74), orange-tip (12,94), pochard (72), pyramidal orchid (58), quaking-grass (90), reserve pictures (front cover, 4,6, 7,8,9,11,14,18,22,24,28,31,32,34,38,40,42,46,48,50,52,56,58, 60,62,64,66,67,70,72,74,76,78,80,82,84,86,88,90,92,93,94, 95,96,97,98,99,100,101,102,103,104,105,106,107,108,109, 110, membership form), ringlet (70), ruddy darter (28), semifree morel (78), shaggy scalycap (18), silver-washed fritillary (28), silverweed (88), sloes (70), sneezewort (18), southern hawker (34), spindle berries (52), toad (34), traveller's-joy (58), tufted duck (66,107,113), wavy bladderwort (24), white admiral (42,60), white-letter hairstreak (60), white spindles (22), wild privet (62), wild strawberry (72), wood anemone (58), wood-sorrel (86), yellow bird's-nest (38), yellow iris (24)

© J. Russell
Kestrel (90)

© D. Smith
Common frog (50), kingfisher (7), mute swan (34,110), robin (116), song thrush (116)

© G. Sowman
Brimstone (2)

© S. Stroud
Elephant hawkmoth (26)

© A. Tasker
Parkridge Centre (112)

© H. Taylor
Little owl (29)

© C. Thomas
Reserve picture (54)

© Warwickshire Wildlife Trust
Barn owl (66), brown hare (52), fieldfare (84), great crested grebe (14), great crested newt (38), great spotted woodpecker (12,64,116), jay (78), lapwing (3,46), stoat (46)

© A. Wincott
Blackcap (60), bullfinch (38), redwing (62), reed warbler (15,54, membership form), treecreeper (front cover, 4,76), water rail (14)

Help protect wildlife ...

In Shakespeare's time, Warwickshire's countryside was very different from today.

There were more woods, meadows, ponds and hedgerows – all vital places for the survival of wildlife.

Today our growing population has changed most of the land to provide more houses, more roads and more industry. Even the fields have been changed to produce more food, using fertilisers and pesticides.

The changes have destroyed many vital habitats needed for wildlife to survive. Not all has been lost, however, and with your help a lot more can be saved.

Join us as a member ... Introduce a new member ... Help us with a donation ... Remember us in your will.

With your support, we can do so much more.

... Join us today

Yes, I would like to join

Members: Why not pass this form on to a friend or give membership as a gift?

Name(s) ______________________

Address ______________________

______________________ Postcode ______________________

*Tel ______________________ *Email ______________________

giftaid it **Please make your gift worth more!**

☐ I wish Warwickshire Wildlife Trust to treat all donations I make from the date of this declaration as Gift Aid donations, until I notify you otherwise. I understand that the tax reclaimed by the Trust (currently 28p in the £1) must not exceed the total amount of Income or Capital Gains Tax which I pay in any tax year.

Signed ______________________

Date ______________ ☐ Please tick here if you do not pay tax.

Minimum subscription
(please tick appropriate box)

Individual ☐ **£24 p.a.** or ☐ **(£2.00/month)**

Joint ☐ **£30 p.a.** or ☐ **(£2.50/month)**

Family with Watch Junior Club
☐ **£36 p.a.** or ☐ **(£3.00/month)**
(for family memberships please attach children's names and DOB's)

Concessionary ☐ **£18 p.a.** or ☐ **(£1.50/month)**

Concessionary Joint ☐ **£22 p.a.** or ☐ **(£1.83/month)**

Registered charity no 209200

VAT no 670 3187 40

Please complete the Direct Debit mandate below or contact us for other payment options

Warwickshire Wildlife Trust — The Wildlife Trusts

Instruction to your Bank or Building Society to pay by Direct Debit

DIRECT Debit

Please fill in the form and send it to Warwickshire Wildlife Trust, Brandon Marsh Nature Centre, Brandon Lane, Coventry CV3 3GW.

Originators Identification Number

8	5	4	2	6	6

To the Manager (Bank or Building Society) ______________________

Address ______________________

____

______________________ Postcode ______________________

Name(s) of Account Holder(s) ______________________

Branch Sort Code ☐☐☐☐☐☐ Account Number ☐☐☐☐☐☐☐☐

Instruction to your Bank or Building Society
Please pay the Warwickshire Wildlife Trust Direct Debits from the account detailed in this instruction subject to the safeguards assured by the Direct Debit Guarantee. I understand that this instruction may remain with the Warwickshire Wildlife Trust and, if so, details will be passed electronically to my Bank/Building Society.

Ref number (office use only) ☐☐☐☐☐☐☐☐

Signature(s) ______________________ Date ______________

Banks and Building Societies may not accept Direct Debit Instructions for some types of account

☐ Warwickshire Wildlife Trust will retain your details on computer and from time to time will contact you about the work of the Trust or direct marketing. If you do not wish to be contacted please tick the box

* By supplying these details you are consenting to being contacted by telephone or email with the above information.

What future for Warwickshire's Wildlife?

Many of us share a deep concern for the fate of our planet after our lifetimes, and the world that will be inherited by our children's children. Threats such as global warming, building developments, intensive agriculture and road construction loom large on the horizon and threaten wildlife habitats on our own doorstep.

Warwickshire Wildlife Trust is committed to protecting Warwickshire's unique wildlife heritage for the future, but to succeed in the long term we need to be able to plan ahead. The Trust has been extremely fortunate in the legacies it has been bequeathed in recent years, which have enabled us to build the foundations for protecting precious wildlife havens for many years to come.

What can a legacy can do for our county's wildlife?

The Ryton Wood Legacy

When Ryton Wood was awarded SSSI (Site of Special Scientific Interest) status in 1984, it went straight to the top of Warwickshire Wildlife Trust's wish list of sites. A year later a large legacy enabled the Trust to purchase the wood for £100,000. Now, after 20 years of positive woodland management, the reserve is thriving.

Ryton Wood is the largest ancient woodland in Warwickshire, a stronghold of 200–300 year old oak trees and the endangered small-leaved lime, a remnant of the last ice age. Thirty-three of Warwickshire's 35 butterfly species inhabit the reserve, including the endangered wood white.

Today, the importance of Ryton Wood has even more value than simply protecting the wood itself. Ryton Wood is at the heart of a project designed to link a number of woodland sites across the Princethorpe landscape and has a critical role in improving the wildlife value of south east Warwickshire. Because the wood is so large it acts as a 'reservoir' or sanctuary for rare species from which recolonisation can begin to occur along wildlife corridors, such as hedgerows and field margins, to nearby woods.

The case of Ryton Wood demonstrates the lasting impact a legacy can have. Because of one individual's passion for wildlife, the future of this precious woodland is guaranteed and is at the centre of a project that aims to re-establish Warwickshire's lost woodlands. More legacies could enable us to buy more land in the area when it becomes available so we can create a stable large woodland area that is viable in the long term.

How your bequest can help

There are a number of ways you can remember Warwickshire's Wildlife in your will, no matter how large or small.

- A fixed sum (pecuniary) legacy where you specify an amount you would like to bequeath
- A residual legacy is another option, where you can bequeath a percentage of your estate
- Requesting donations in lieu of flowers at the funeral

Legacies can help us to:

- Provide protection for endangered species
- Buy and manage nature reserves and landscapes
- Educate and inspire our children
- Encourage volunteers to help conserve local areas

Please help us by taking the next step...

☐ **Please send me my FREE booklet about leaving a legacy**

☐ **I am considering leaving a Legacy to Warwickshire Wildlife Trust and would like someone to contact me to discuss it further**

☐ **I have already remembered Warwickshire Wildlife Trust in my will**

Title: Mr/Mrs/Ms/Other ______ Name ________________________________

Address ________________________________

____

________________________________ Postcode ______________

*Telephone ________________________________

*Email ________________________________

Please return to:

Warwickshire Wildlife Trust
FREEPOST NAT19399
COV... RY
C...

...Vildlife Trust will retain your details on computer and from time to time will contact you about the work of the Trust ...ng. If you do not wish to be contacted please tick the box

...you are consenting to being contacted by telephone or email with the above information.

...counts